Editor
Dona Herweck Rice

Editorial Project Manager
Dona Herweck Rice

Editor-in-Chief
Sharon Coan, M.S. Ed.

Art Coordinator
Denice Adorno

Imaging
Alfred Lau

Product Manager
Phil Garcia

Publishers
Rachelle Cracchiolo, M.S. Ed.
Mary Dupuy Smith, M.S. Ed.

Grammar, Usage & Mechanics

Level 7

Author

Karen Alexander

Teacher Created Materials, Inc.
6421 Industry Way
Westminster, CA 92683
www.teachercreated.com

ISBN-0-7439-3570-5

©*2001 Teacher Created Materials, Inc.*
Made in U.S.A.

The classroom teacher may reproduce copies of materials in this book for classroom use only. The reproduction of any part for an entire school or school system is strictly prohibited. No part of this publication may be transmitted, stored, or recorded in any form without written permission from the publisher.

Grammar, Usage, and Mechanics

A nonfiction reading & writing program • A nonfiction reading & writing program

Table of Contents

Sentence Structure 3
Sentence Structure General Information—Simple, Compound, and Complex Sentences—How Many Ways Are There To Write This Anyway?—Revision Do's and Do Not's—Do the Practice—You Mean There's More?—Ready, Set, Action!—Scwewy Sentences—No More Scwewy Sentences!

Grammar and Punctuation 13
Capitalization—Capitalization Practice—Punctuation Marks—Punctuation Practice—More Punctuation Practice—Leftover Hodgepodge

Parts of Speech 23
Parts-of-Speech General Information—Nouns—Noun Search—Pronouns—Pronoun Practice—Proper Pronoun Usage—Crazy Cases—Verbs—Verb Curb—Verbacious Sentences—Adjectives and Adverbs—This Is More Interesting!—Descriptive Quilt—Adjective and Adverb Use—Prepositions, Conjunctions, and Interjections—Construction Zone—Sort 'Em

Spelling 42
Spelling Helps—Now That Your Head Is Spinning, Spell It—More Spelling Rules: Who Made Up This Stuff?—Spell It ~~Write~~ Right

English Usage 47
Agreement—To Agree or Not To Agree—Writing It Right—Irregular Plurals—That's Some Story!—Blast From the Past—Root Words—Prefixes First, Suffixes Last—First and Last—New Words—Number Usage—1, 2, 3, Go!

Paragraphs 62
About Paragraphs—Beware of the Body Snatchers!—Entirely Irrelevant and Out of Order

Student Papers 66
Summaries and Outlines—Outspoken Outlines—Compositions and Essays—Research Papers—Research Assignment

Answer Key 71

Note to the Teacher

This entire *Grammar, Usage, & Mechanics* manual has been designed to be used in the order it has been presented. Use it in its entirety for a thorough overview of the skills, or simply review those sections which apply to your current needs.

Grammar, Usage, and Mechanics

A nonfiction reading & writing program • A nonfiction reading & writing program

Sentence Structure General Information

To be effective, sentences must communicate facts and ideas in a manner that shows the relationship between them. Written in sequence, those sentences enable a good writer to express him or herself clearly in an interesting manner. An inexperienced writer often creates weak sentences that do not allow for clear, reasoned ideas. A good writer will revise these sentences carefully by first rethinking them and then by rearranging them.

example of weak sentences and sequence: Bugs scare me. Flowers make me sneeze. But I still enjoy the country.

revised sentence: Though I enjoy the country, bugs scare me and flowers make me sneeze.

other revised sentence: I enjoy the country; however, bugs scare me and flowers make me sneeze.

There are many possible revisions for each sentence. The writer must determine which revision is most effective for his or her paper.

Types of Sentences

There are three types of sentences: *simple*, *compound*, and *complex*.

The **simple sentence** has one subject and one verb. It can take the forms of *declarative* (ending with a period), *exclamatory* (ending with an exclamation point), or *interrogative* (ending with a question mark).

example of a simple declarative sentence: The cat ran.

with a compound subject added: The cat and the dog ran.

with a compound verb added: The cat ran and leapt up a tree.

No punctuation is needed to separate subjects and verbs in simple sentences.

The **complex sentence** has two parts, each with its own verb. Each part is called a clause. One clause is complete, and it is called a main clause. The other clause, the subordinate or dependent clause, cannot stand alone. If the main clause comes first, no punctuation is needed to separate the two sentences.

example: Wendy can fly if Tinkerbell sprinkles pixie dust on her.

If the subordinate clause comes first, it is followed by a comma. A subordinate clause interrupts the main idea and makes no sense alone.

example: If Tinkerbell sprinkles pixie dust on Wendy, she will be able to fly.

Connecting words that used most frequently at the beginning of dependent clauses are the following: *that, when, if, which, who, after, until, because, before, once, since, so, that, although, whenever,* and *while*.

Grammar, Usage, and Mechanics

Sentence Structure
General Information (cont.)

The **compound sentence** differs from the complex sentence in that the compound contains two or more separate, stand-alone sentences. Since they must be joined together, punctuation is needed. Three types of punctuation are used, as follows:

1. a comma to separate sentences, followed by one of seven coordinating conjunctions: *for, and, nor, but, or, yet,* and *so* (Think of the acronym FANBOYS.)

    example: The park is closed, but the activity center down the street is open.

2. a semicolon to separate two sentences

    example: The park is closed; the activity center down the street is open.

3. a semicolon and a transitional word or phrase followed by a comma to separate the sentences (Transitional words include the following: *however, on the other hand, furthermore,* and *nonetheless*.)

    example: The park is closed; however, the activity center down the street is open.

Grammar, Usage, and Mechanics

Simple, Compound, and Complex Sentences

Using pages 3 and 4 as guides, correct the following sentences with a colored pen or pencil. If the sentence is all right as it is, write OK after the sentence. If you make one or more corrections to the sentence, write the reason for each correction after the sentence.

1. My Uncle James isn't a professional but he can dance better than anyone I know.

2. Katie will attend swim lessons and bring her own swim accessories.

3. Because their son was hospitalized the parents also spent the night in the hospital.

4. I cannot believe my parents have imposed a telephone curfew on me I can only talk for an hour a day.

5. He was late and that made me nervous.

6. The principal will be at the meeting tomorrow however the vice-principal will still be in the office.

7. The sixteen-year-old boy has had three accidents in four months: his insurance rates are high.

8. The parade marchers were hot and sweaty nonetheless they were required to continue their one-mile course.

9. She couldn't decide which outfit to wear to the party her clothes were strewn all over the floor.

10. After high school he has the option of going to college with a scholarship on the other hand he could play for a major league baseball team.

11. The toddlers played nicely until one took a toy belonging to the other.

12. The supermarket burnt down last night the market across town is in business however.

13. If you train a horse well it can do many tricks.

14. Some people believe that Humpty Dumpty fell off a wall on the other hand he may have been pushed.

15. The driving age for most states is sixteen years old, however; some states require kids to wait until they turn eighteen.

Grammar, Usage, and Mechanics

How Many Ways Are There To Write This Anyway?

To avoid a boring paper, vary the length and structure of your sentences. Some ideas follow:

A. Begin a sentence with a *prepositional phrase*.

   example: **On a log,** the turtles basked peacefully in the middle of the lagoon and were unaware of the approaching alligator.

B. Begin a sentence with a *verbal phrase*.

   example: **Basking peacefully,** the turtles on the logs, in the middle of the lagoon, were unaware of the approaching alligator.

C. Begin a sentence with an *expletive* (the word *it* or *there* used to introduce a sentence in which the subject follows the verb).

   example: **There** were turtles in the middle of the lagoon basking peacefully on a log, unaware of the approaching alligator.

D. Begin a sentence with a *subordinate clause*.

   example: **As they basked peacefully on the logs in the middle of the lagoon,** the turtles were unaware of the approaching alligator.

E. You can also change the style of the sentence by using the *interrogative* (asking a question) or *imperative* (expressing a command or request) forms of sentences.

   example of an interrogative sentence: Where were the turtles? On a log in the middle of the lagoon, completely unaware of the approaching alligator.

   example of an imperative sentence: Look out, little turtles! Stop basking in the lagoon as if everything is peaceful and fine. Look around; an alligator is fast approaching!

On another sheet of paper, rewrite each of the following sentences twice, varying the structure in two of the ways suggested above.

1. We came home cranky and exhausted after a two-hour drive from the beach.
2. Our dogs got loose, but were brought home by our ever-patient neighbor.
3. The carpenter, his mouth full of nails and his steel hammer swinging like a piece of machinery, nailed and put together the toy box with amazing precision.
4. The frugal mother bought only second-hand clothing for her baby at the consignment store and was able to afford a beautiful, hardly worn, extensive wardrobe.
5. The P.E. teacher rushed onto the field to assist an injured player.
6. He knew he was in the beginning stages of illness because his body ached and his head pounded.
7. The singer swayed back and forth to the rhythm of the song, like a wheat field on a dry, windy day.
8. The tsunami caused much devastation on the island of Hawaii; the mainland states were quick to offer assistance.
9. They wanted to go to the beach to meet their friends, but the beach was closed due to an oil spill.
10. The child ran to the man she thought was her father and gave him a hug, not realizing he was a stranger.

Grammar, Usage, and Mechanics

A nonfiction reading & writing program • A nonfiction reading & writing program

Revision Do's and Do Not's

Sentences can be grammatically perfect and clear, but still not be effective. Effectiveness requires the skill to rethink and revise what you want to say in an interesting way that gives full meaning to your ideas.

The following do's and do not's are basic "rules" of sentence writing that guide you to building strong sentences and tell you where your sentences may go wrong.

A. **Do** repeat key words and ideas often for emphasis.
   example: It is true that you may *fool* all the people some of the time; you can even *fool* some of the people all of the time; but you can't *fool* all of the people all of the time. (Abraham Lincoln)

B. **Do not** repeat other types of words too often or you will weaken your sentence.
   example: *In my opinion*, the poor always *seem* to be housed in broken, run-down neighborhoods, are *seeming* to fight off debt, are worried, it *seems*, by an increasing economy, and *in my opinion*, are barely able to survive.

C. **Do** use a thesaurus, a synonym guide, or a dictionary to find just the right word to express your idea.

D. **Do** be careful in using the words *always, never, all, none, right*, and *wrong*. Using these words in statements without collecting and presenting ample evidence for your opinion is a careless mistake.

E. **Do** use, instead, the word *seldom* in place of *never* and *usually, regularly,* or *likely* in place of *always*.

F. **Do not** be wordy. Get to the point.
   example: When the time came to go home, he left.
   revised: When it was time, he left.

G. **Do not** use slang, non-standard language, or clichés.
   example of slang: My teacher is the thing. He rocks.
   example of non-standard language: I don't want no peas for dinner.
   example of a cliché: He's the big man on campus.

H. **Do** arrange ideas in a series in order of their increasing importance.
   example: The skateboarder lost his balance, fell, and cracked a rib.

I. **Do not** write *and* too many times in a sentence. This is repetitive and rather boring.

J. **Do not** use the "primer style" (a series of short, simple sentences) throughout your paper. This makes your work boring and monotonous.
   example: He walked to the market. The wind was blowing hard. He could barely stand up. He saw a tornado. It hit the market.
   revised: Trudging towards the market through he howling wind, the boy witnessed the awesome power of a killer tornado as it struck and demolished the object of his destination.

K. **Do** write enough concise details to explain your point clearly to your readers.

L. **Do not** use unessential details that cause the reader to be sidetracked and confused.

M. **Do not** omit important information that is evident to you, the writer, but not to your reader.

©Teacher Created Materials, Inc.

Grammar, Usage, and Mechanics

Do the Practice

Rewrite the following sentences on another piece of paper according to the appropriate **Do** or **Do Not** rules suggested on the previous page.

1. He approached the horse warily. The horse saw the bridle in his hand. The boy stood still. The horse waited. He tried to toss the reins over the horse's head. But he missed the horse. The horse ran away. *(Rewrite with rules B and J in mind.)*

2. My car, which I bought from a friend of mine, a car lover, who buys old problem cars and then fixes them, always perfectly, as a hobby, had begun a rumbling problem in the car's engine which has begun to worry me for I know nothing about problems with cars and I never have money to go to a car repairman. *(Rewrite with rules B, C, D, E, F, and L in mind.)*

3. Bubble gum chewing, without your teacher knowing you have it, is cool, except when you get caught with it stuck all over your nose from a popped bubble, and when you sneak it, and when your teacher suddenly sees you chewing in class. *(Rewrite with rules F, G, H, and I in mind)*

4. I got up very early this morning. I took a long shower. I dawdled while eating breakfast. I changed outfits four times because I couldn't make up my mind which one to wear. Then the bus came and I was in my underwear. *(Rewrite with rule J in mind.)*

5. The space trip was a success, but the astronauts were kept in seclusion for weeks afterward to guard them against the infection. *(Rewrite with rules K and M in mind.)*

Writer's Contest

Create a lengthy, descriptive, and effective sentence or two about the mishaps of a substitute teacher. Since this is a contest, the sentences will be judged by your teacher on originality, creativity, and effectiveness. The best sentence will be awarded first prize. (The question is, can you wheedle a prize from your teacher?)

Grammar, Usage, and Mechanics

A nonfiction reading & writing program • A nonfiction reading & writing program

You Mean There's More?

Most effective sentences join two or more relating ideas by *coordination* (expressing equality of ideas) or *subordination* (expressing inequality of ideas). Coordinating ideas are joined with the words *and*, *or*, or *but*.

    example: She is nice and sweet.

Subordinate ideas, being less important, need to be written first in a series (see rule H on page 6) or need to be interjected in the sentence within commas.

    poor example: Walt Disney was a very creative man and designed and built Disneyland in 1955.

    revised: Walt Disney, a creative man, designed and built Disneyland in 1955.

Parallelism, another means for creating effective sentences, helps clarify sentences by using similar word structure throughout them. For example, sentences written in the past tense should not have future or present tense mixed with them.

    poor example: We are camping. And we went to the river yesterday. Soon we'll climb a mountain.

To revise, use a parallel structure diagram.

    camping
    rafting   } are three things we are doing.
    climbing

or

    to camp
    to raft   } are what we like to do.
    to climb

    revision: While camping, we went river rafting and mountain climbing.

Parallelism also sets a similar pattern for combining ideas.

    awkward example: She loves to dance and singing.

    parallel 1: She loves dancing and singing.

    parallel 2: She loves to dance and to sing.

    parallel 3: She loves to dance and sing.

To become a more successful writer, emphasize your ideas in a direct manner. To do so, use the *active voice* (putting the subject first, followed by an active verb and then the object) over the *passive voice* (putting the receiver in front, then the verb, and finally the subject).

    passive example: The dog was hit by a car.

    active example: The car hit the dog.

Grammar, Usage, and Mechanics

A nonfiction reading & writing program • A nonfiction reading & writing program

Ready, Set, Action!

A. One a separate sheet of paper, use the following word prompts to create active, complete, parallel, and effective sentences.

1. thinned hair
   freckled face
   stooped posture

2. the results are mind-boggling
   surprising
   shocking

3. ridiculous talent show
   hilarious

4. reverberating
   thundering
   clashing

5. ferocious monster
   vicious

6. inheritance of a million dollars
   furniture
   six dogs

B. On a separate sheet of paper, express the coordinate ideas in the following sentences in parallel structure.

1. The parents were told that for enrolling their children in kindergarten they need to obtain doctor's shot records and that then they could be filling out the school paperwork.

2. My teacher not only works full-time, but she is involving herself in the P.T.A., goes to graduate school, and doing her own housework.

3. Our school committee voted to replace our portables with ones that have more room and having air-conditioning.

4. To be a good policeman, one must be upholding the law, level headed amidst unpredictable circumstances, liking to help others, and keeping in good physical shape.

5. Our Boy Scout leader is effective because he's honest, being funny, and speaking better than anyone I know.

Grammar, Usage, and Mechanics

Scwewy Sentences

A *fragment* is any group of words that is set off as a sentence but lacks a subject, a verb, or main clause. Because fragments are usually improperly punctuated parts of an adjacent sentence, they can almost always be revised by joining them to that sentence, although other revisions may also be needed.

example: When the skater broke his arm. It was a broken skateboard wheel that caused the accident.

revised: When the skater broke his arm, it was a broken skateboard wheel that caused the accident.

A *run-on sentence* omits punctuation between main clauses. The run-on is the result of two grammatically complete thoughts in the same sentence. To revise add 1) a period, 2) a comma and a coordinating conjunction, 3) a semi-colon, or 4) change one of the main clauses to a subordinate clause.

example: My dad thinks he's so funny his sense of humor is an embarrassment to me.

revision 1: My dad thinks he's so funny. His sense of humor is an embarrassment to me.

revision 2: My dad thinks he's so funny, but his sense of humor is an embarrassment to me.

revision 3: My dad thinks he's so funny; his sense of humor is an embarrassment to me.

revision 4: Although my dad thinks he's so funny, his sense of humor is an embarrassment to me.

Faulty pronoun reference occurs when pronoun antecedents are not obvious or clear.

ambiguous example: Jane told Sally that she is happy with her.

Who was happy with whom? It is completely unclear to whom the writer is referring.

Faulty predication refers to carelessly constructed sentences that combine verbs and subjects that do not fit together.

faulty example: My cat is a reason some people don't own pets. She sheds on our furniture, claws it to pieces, and sometimes even urinates in it!

"My cat is a reason" makes no sense. Rewrite the sentences to read, "The behavior of my cat is a reason . . . ."

Sometimes revision is not possible if the subject is so vague it cannot be clarified.

example: Drugs are a serious quarrel today.

Here we are not sure what is meant. Perhaps the writer meant to say that the war on drugs causes serious quarrels between politicians and citizens. Who can really say, except the author? Clarification by revision, using more concise words, is definitely needed.

Mixed constructions occur when a writer begins a sentence in one construction and then shifts to another. This results in a sentence that is so wordy the writer becomes confused and loses track of the subject and which verb complements it.

example: The fact that John was a good worker he had many offers to obtain good jobs.

revised: Because John was a good worker, he had many job offers.

Grammar, Usage, and Mechanics

A nonfiction reading & writing program • A nonfiction reading & writing program

No More Scwewy Sentences!

Read each faulty sentence. Before each sentence, write one of the following to show the error:

    F for fragment
    R for run-on
    FPR for faulty pronoun reference
    FP for faulty predications
    MC for mixed constructions.

Then, on a separate sheet of paper, rewrite the sentences correctly.

_____ 1. The magician's first trick was a length of rope.

_____ 2. I think we should ignore the gang. Or leave quickly.

_____ 3. Jake has a bunny with ear mites which he is always scratching.

_____ 4. In every effort the foreigner made to make himself understood got him more confused and failed to succeed.

_____ 5. The dentist finally called me in. To conference with me about dental health.

_____ 6. Another kind of crime is dishonesty.

_____ 7. Having spent such great sums for campaign endorsements has left the government with fewer resources to help the sick and elderly.

_____ 8. Lewis and Clark gazed upon the canyon their mouths dropped in awe.

_____ 9. The rainbows shined brightly over the rich field of flowers. They were of many colors.

_____ 10. As the center for most T.V. studios, most young actors, actresses and models yearn to go to Hollywood.

Challenge

Sentences with faulty pronoun references can be rather humorous. Write three of them. Be creative and funny. Trade your work with a classmate and have him or her edit and correct the faulty sentences.

    example: The turtle eyed me, riding my bicycle.
    revised: The turtle eyed me as I rode my bicycle.

Grammar, Usage, and Mechanics

A nonfiction reading & writing program • A nonfiction reading & writing program

Capitalization

I've been learning this stuff since I was in kindergarten! Why do I have to study this again, you may ask? Because students your age still tend to make careless errors in this area. You've heard the old saying, "Practice makes perfect." So, let's practice and get it right!

To capitalize you begin a word with an uppercase letter. Here is a list of the kinds of words you should always capitalize.

the word *I*
> Under no circumstances will I break my promise to you.

the first word in a sentence
> Learning to use grammar is my idea of fun.

the names of people, races, and nationalities (*proper nouns*)
> Pam E. Jones
> Aborigine
> Cherokee

words derived from proper nouns (*proper adjectives*)
> Australian
> New Yorker

titles with people's names (*titles of position, rank, etc.*)
> Governor Davis
> Mr. Lopez
> Dr. Finkenschweigel
> Captain Kirk

names of places (*proper nouns*)
> Mississippi River
> the South
> Adams Elementary School

brand names
> Kleenex
> Old Navy
> Skittles

days of the week and months
> Monday
> March
> December

Grammar, Usage, and Mechanics

Capitalization (cont.)

the first letter of each word in a friendly letter greeting and in a one-word closing
    Dear Grandma,
    Love,
    Yours,

the first letter of each word in a business letter greeting and in a one-word closing
    To Whom It May Concern:
    Dear Sir:
    Sincerely,

specific organizations, historical events, and documents
    Declaration of Independence
    Korean War
    Daughters of the American Revolution

the main words in titles of books, movies, newspapers, television shows, plays, operas, musicals, or magazines
    The Lion, the Witch, and the Wardrobe
    The New York Times
    Star Wars

school subjects if they are languages or actual class titles listed in a catalog
    Spanish
    Geometry II
    Underwater Basket Weaving

holidays
    Mother's Day
    Christmas
    Yom Kippur

Here are some situations when you should not capitalize.
person's title when not used with a name or in place of a name
    I will write to Sam Smithberg, the president of Bank of America.
    My uncle won the state lottery.
    Is your dad going to the game?

the four seasons	regular school subjects	geographical locations
winter	social studies	Go west until you come to the highway.
spring	language arts	We'll head south now.
autumn	physical education	The birds flew east of the river.

Grammar, Usage, and Mechanics

Capitalization Practice

Using a colored pen or pencil, edit the capitalization errors in the following sentences by capitalizing words as necessary and removing unnecessary capitals.

1. After leaving newport beach, we sailed west toward Catalina island for our Summer vacation with my Cousins and uncle john.

2. Dr. Martin Luther King, jr., first gained Public awareness as a Leader in the civil rights sit-ins in the south.

3. The U.S. congress is made of the house of representatives and the senate, which is elected every two years, to pass national laws.

4. I took a Chemistry course in my Freshman year in High School in Nebraska, and i was a college Graduate student five years later.

5. Last Summer we attended vacation bible school at Grant park, Northwest of Grant elementary school.

6. Though I've never seen *phantom of the opera*, my grandmother told me that the african american man who plays the Phantom is incredibly talented.

7. We went to hear the Choir at the Community College last Saturday. Some of the songs they sang were Traditional, some were from popular movies, and a few were Patriotic. They sang a wonderful rendition of "the battle hymn of the republic."

8. I'll never forget last labor day when my sister was actually in labor giving birth to her First-Born son at san antonio hospital.

9. I'm driving the new ford to ralph's market to purchase coca-cola, toilet paper, soda crackers, oreo cookies, and fruit loops.

10. My Father is the president of toys r' us. He can get great deals on things like pokemon videos, game boy cartridges, skate boards, bikes, and mattel products.

Challenge
Write a short story and intentionally leave words lowercase that should be capitalized. Include in your story one sample of each capitalization rule from pages 12 and 13. Exchange with a fellow student and edit one another's story.

Grammar, Usage, and Mechanics

A nonfiction reading & writing program • A nonfiction reading & writing program

Punctuation Marks

Just to be certain you know what you are doing when it comes to punctuation, review the information on these four pages. You can use the informatioin to help you with the worksheets that follow.

, This is a comma. Here is how to use it:
- to indicate a pause between adjectives, clauses, phrases, or sentences
  example: Let's eat, Mom. (Without a comma this would read, "Let's eat mom.")
- to separate a city and state
  example: Boston, Massachusetts
- to separate a date and year
  example: December 31, 1999
- to separate every three numerals within a large number starting from the right
  example: 1,543,785
- to separate two or more words in a list or series
  example: I ate two corn dogs, some pizza, a hamburger, and french fries.
- to set off an appositive phrase
  example: Michael Jordan, the greatest basketball player ever, is speaking at my school.
- after introductory words at the beginning of a sentence
  example: After climbing a mile up the mountain, he sat against a log in the shade to rest.
- around interrupters
  example: The delegates and representatives, of course, will show up at the convention.
- after the name of a person to whom someone is speaking
  example: Juan, are you buying into another high interest investment plan?
- to separate a quotation tag from a quotation
  example: Juan replied, "Yes, I've bought into five already. I'm going to be rich someday."
- to separate a quote from any interruption the writer wishes to interject
  example: "I am going on vacation," he stated enthusiastically, "in just one week!"
- after a greeting or closing in a letter to a friend or relative
  example: Dear Grandpa, *or* Sincerely,

This is an apostrophe. Here is how to use it:
- in contractions
  examples: it's (it is), we'll (we will*)*
- to indicate possession unless using the word "its"
  examples: Katie's nose, *or* It's an alligator and it can't find <u>its</u> way out of our pool!
- in singular words that end in "s" (Add another "s" unless pronunciation is too difficult.)
  examples: James's book, Wes's convertible, *but* Moses' rod, not Moses's rod
- in plural words that already end in "s" (Add only the apostrophe at the end of the word.)
  example: the boys' bikes

Grammar, Usage, and Mechanics

Punctuation Marks (cont.)

( ) **These are parentheses.** Here is how to use them:
- around words or phrases that add information or make an idea clearer
  example: The green-eyed monster (my sister) is away this weekend.

[ ] **These are brackets.** Here is how to use them.
- to correct editorial errors, typos, and misspellings in an original text that is being misquoted
  example: He is later [than] usual. (The original text said *then*.)
- to add needed or clarifying information left out of the original text, as in speech
  example: It was a [political] scenario.Ω

• **This is a colon.** Here is how to use it:
- after the greeting in the business letter
  example: Dear Mr. Okasaki: *and* To Whom It May Concern:
- to introduce a list
  example: Please bring the following items: lined paper, colored pencils, and markers.
- between the hour and minutes in the time of day
  example: 7:30 A.M.
- to introduce an important point when one sentence explains the sentence next to it
  example: Lockers are all over the school, but some aren't for students: those by room #2 are only for teachers.

" " **These are quotation marks.** Here is how to use them:
- at the beginning and end of a direct quote
  example: "You're driving me nuts," she complained.
- to enclose a quote within a quote (Note: Use a single quotation mark.)
  example: She said to her son, "You know your father always says, 'Treat others as you wish to be treated.' "
- when you want to draw attention to a special word usage, clause, or title
  examples: Is this what you call "acceptable"? My brother is the "Gross Out King."
- at the beginning and end of the titles of songs, short poems, chapters of books, and television and radio programs (unless in a continuing series)
  examples: On television's "Superstar Football Special," he sang "The Star Spangled Banner." *or* I am reading a short story in our literature text, "To Build a Fire," by Jack London.

Note: For punctuation that does not belong to the title itself but is needed in the sentence, place a comma or period inside the quotation marks and a colon, semi-colon, question mark, and exclamation point outside of them.

Punctuation Marks (cont.)

- **This is a period.** Here is how to use it:
  - at the end of a declarative sentence
    example: I decided to relax in the hammock.
  - after abbreviations
    examples: Dr. *or* etc.

- **This is the question mark.** Here is how to use it:
  - at the end of interrogative sentences (questions)
    example: Have you ever spent the night in a tree house?
  - inside the quotes when someone asks a question
    example: "How much does this cost?" he asked.
  - outside the quotes when a question is asked about the quoted material
    example: Who said, "The car is broken"?
  - inside the quotes when a question is asked about quoted material *and* the quoted material itself is a question
    example: Who said, "Is the car broken again?"

  Note: Do not use a question mark at the end of an indirect question.
  example: I wonder what I'll look like when I grow up.

- **This is an exclamation mark.** Here is how to use it:
  - to show strong feeling after a word, a phrase, or an exclamatory sentence
    example: Oh no! My underwear just flew out the window!

  Note: Do not overuse exclamation points, and never use multiple exclamation points all in a row!!!!

- **This is a hyphen.** Here is how to use it:
  - to break a word between syllables at the end of a line
    example: My sister wants to eat lob-
    ster on her birthday.
  - between two-part numbers
    example: fifty-two
  - when writing fractions as words
    example: one-half
  - to join two words that become one adjective
    example: The computer game is user-friendly.

Punctuation Marks (cont.)

- to form some compound words
  examples: short-term, one-day-old baby
- to avoid an awkward grouping of letters
  example: cell-like (as opposed to celllike)
- to distinguish between root words with the prefixes *self-, all-, ex-,* and the suffix *-elect*
  examples: self-centered, all-important, ex-wife, re-elect
- in double "a" or double "i" words
  example: anti-inflammatory

— This is a dash. Here is how to use it:

- to indicate a sudden break in a sentence
  example: I was in my garden—my brother calls it my weed patch—where I found three cocoons.
- when you are already using a colon and do not want to use it twice in a sentence
  example: Here's another ad from our competition—our delicious restaurants can be found all over the city: on Main St., Second St., Euclid Ave., and Harbor Boulevard.
- in dialogue to interrupt a speech
  example: "I was wondering—when he asked about the report, why did he want to know?"
- in a sentence to add another thought and or idea, when one has already been expressed
  example: He is lucky to have made it—even to be alive.

... This is an ellipsis. Here is how to use it:

- to replace words that have been left out or to indicate a pause
  example: Hmmmm . . . now that I think about it . . . maybe aliens did visit my brother.

; This is a semicolon. Here is how to use it:

- to join independent clauses of a compound sentence (when not using both a comma and a conjunction) when those clauses can be broken down into two complete thoughts
  example: I have a new baby brother; I can't wait to see him!
- in front of a subordinating conjunction when joining two simple sentences
  example: Larry apologized to Mrs. Harris; however, she kept screaming anyway.
- in a series of three or more items when commas are used within those items
  example: Our talent show has been planned. We will have Jazz, a group of dancers; Klutzy Kyle, a magical extravaganza; Barkinov, a poodle that dances ballet; and Spring Showers, a folk singer.

Grammar, Usage, and Mechanics

Punctuation Practice

Use a colored pen or pencil to add commas, colons, semicolon, hyphens, and dashes correctly in each sentence.

1. Many young boys hope to become professional sportsmen however few realize the amount of work necessary not to mention the luck involved in becoming a success.

2. Some people feel that American public schools should only be taught in English not Spanish nevertheless some schools do still have waivers for bilingual education not just English.

3. When the test was placed in front of him he realized dreading his upcoming report card how much more he should have studied.

4. The vice president of the company boasts that he is self made and self educated but his boasting which occurs every time he opens his mouth shows his self centeredness.

5. There are three types of government the federal state and local.

6. I have to be at the Chess Club meeting after school we're taking pictures for our class bulletin board the Tyler School yearbook and *The Evening Press Newspaper*.

7. Delighted to hold his one day old son the new father burst into tears of joy amazed beyond words at the priceless miracle he'd received.

8. After selling off all his old things at the garage sale he sat and thought about what he had gotten rid of the books his grandmother had bought him his race car sets the train set his dad and he had bought together and model cars everything sentimental was it really worth the small amount of money he had made he wondered.

9. Its easy to borrow money its much more difficult to pay it back.

10. Some say that America is taking over the world not necessarily with world power and force but with the use of media through television, film, radio, and the press.

Grammar, Usage, and Mechanics

More Punctuation Practice

A. Using a colored pen or pencil, insert periods, question marks, exclamations, and ellipses into the following quote from the Native American, Tecumesh, of the Shawnee Tribe. (Remember that ellipses replace missing text.)

"Where today are the Pequot   Where are the Narragansett   and many other once powerful tribes of our people   They have vanished before the avarice and the oppression of the White Man, as snow before a summer sun

Will we let ourselves be destroyed in our turn without a struggle, give up our homes, our country bequeathed to us by the Great Spirit, the graves of our own dead   I know you will cry with me, 'Never Never ' "

B. Using a colored pen or pencil, insert periods, question marks, and exclamation points into the following paragraph.

James W Marshall was the first man to find gold in California in 1848 at Sutter's Mill Word of the find eventually spread like wildfire   "Gold   Gold   There's gold in them, there hills " prospectors shouted   San Francisco virtually became a ghost town overnight   Miners could earn as much as seventy-five dollars a day, as opposed to the six dollars a month they had been earning on average before the stike   Entrepreneurs asked themselves if selling supplies might be more profitable than mining for gold   These entrepreneurs got rich overnight by selling flour, sugar, coffee, shovels, picks, pans, and more to the miners at incredibly high prices   In addition, gold fever swept the nation with epidemic speed, and California's population rose drastically because of it   Was this one of America's most noted periods in history   Some historians believe so

Grammar, Usage, and Mechanics

A nonfiction reading & writing program • A nonfiction reading & writing program

Leftover Hodgepodge

In the following sentences, determine whether grammar and punctuation marks are used correctly or incorrectly, and what additional grammar and punctuation marks are needed. Revise each sentence that requires corrections. Write the reasons for all of your decisions.

1. Ive seen Broadway's *cat's* twice; and i still find it's musical choreography exciting, well done and original

2. People of all races must learn to live and work together without prejudice; otherwise, this country will fail.

3. I wondered why I received an un-expected letter from the Director of the internal Revenue service could I have done something wrong, I pondered? It turned out simply to be a reminder to sign the form i had sent.

4. Does anyone know who said ive never met a man i did'nt like? I think it Will Rogers a friend to all men.

5. Our family enjoys trip's to Laughlin Nevada for several reasons the boating and skiing on the river the gambling and the dining at the buffets My father likes gambling in all the casinos Harrahs the Flamingo the Hilton you know the rest. He often wins the jackpots. I call him the jackpot king when he plays the slot machines at all those different casinos. The biggest amount he ever won was 8000 and he didn't even share a penny of it with me

Grammar, Usage, and Mechanics

Parts-of-Speech General Information

This chart provides basic information about the function of each part of speech. Use it as a quick reference when building your sentences and looking for ways to enhance them.

Function	Parts of Speech
naming words	**nouns** and **pronouns**
predicating (making a statement or assertion about the subject)	**verbs**
modifying (describing)	**adverbs** and **adjectives**
connecting	**prepositions** and **conjunctions**
mood setting	**interjections**

Nouns and verbs are the main elements in a sentence. Modifying and connecting words expand and refine these basic patterns. Interjections, if used, help to set the mood of the sentences.

Grammar, Usage, and Mechanics

Nouns

Nouns are words that function as the most basic part of a sentence, the subject. A noun is a word which names something: a person, place, thing, or idea.

person: attorney, producer, grandparent, victim

place: Venezuela, arcade, agency, basement

thing: snowman, scrapbook, karaoke, virtual reality

idea: honesty, jealousy, tension, exuberance

There are proper, common, concrete, abstract, and collective nouns.

A *proper noun* is a name of a specific person, place, thing, or idea.

examples of proper nouns: Buzz Lightyear, *Little Women,* Thursday, Florida, President Bush

A *common noun* is a name that is not specific.

examples of common nouns: character, half-pike, videotape, arthropod

A *concrete noun* names something that can be touched and seen.

examples of concrete nouns: sundae, Corvette, Joe Smith, carousel

An *abstract noun* is the name of something that can be talked about but not seen or touched.

examples of abstract nouns: Judaism, happiness, democracy, courage, illness

A *collective noun* is the name of a collection of persons, places, things, or ideas.

examples of collective nouns: United Nations, cluster, litter, assemblage

A *plural noun* is formed in a variety of ways:

- You can usually add "s" at the end to make a noun plural.
  examples: backpacks, photographers

- Some nouns require an "es" added to the end.
  examples: buses, kisses, churches

- There are a few irregular nouns that are made plural by remaining the same, changing one or more letters, or adding letters other than "s" or "es."
  examples: deer, women, children

- Finally, some nouns become plural by adding an "s" to the first word of a noun phrase.
  examples: mothers-in-law, chiefs-of-staff, courts marshall

Grammar, Usage, and Mechanics

A nonfiction reading & writing program • A nonfiction reading & writing program

Noun Search

How many nouns can you find in this wordsearch puzzle? Circle the nouns in the puzzle. Then list each one under its correct category in the chart below.

Proper	Common/Concrete	Abstract	Collective
_____	_____	_____	_____
_____	_____	_____	_____
_____	_____	_____	_____
_____	_____	_____	_____
_____	_____	_____	_____
	_____		

```
I Q X C D I V E G C R C L I Q U E
A M C O N V O Y K A E A Y G F C D
L O P R I N C I P A L P K H D O U
B C A R B D C F V C A A F R H M T
E C O E E Q T L P H X C X J A M I
R U C S W S V N I S M I K Y R I T
T R K P F H S O T Q N T L U R T L
E R C O M E D I A N U Y N C Y E U
I E I N R U R S O B T E D A P E M
N N T D G A T S Y N D V C T O Y Q
S C E E O I N E M R Q Z I A T T U
T E R N C P L S U N A E T N T E E
E G P C X C A B O R I G I N E I A
I K S E N A T O R Y Q O R U R C S
N W H E R I T A G E A I C M T O Y
Y B U R E A C R A C Y L U D L S V
```

Grammar, Usage, and Mechanics

A nonfiction reading & writing program • A nonfiction reading & writing program

Pronouns

Pronouns are words used in place of nouns. The noun for which a pronoun stands is called its *antecedent*. Pronouns can be classified as follows:

Four Cases of Pronouns

	Subjective/ Nominative	Objective	Possessive	Reflexive
Singular 1st person 2nd person 3rd person	I you he, she, it	me you him, her, it	my/mine your/yours his, her/hers, its	myself yourself himself, herself, itself
Plural 1st person 2nd person 3rd person	we you(all) they	us you(all) them	our/ours your/yours their/theirs	ourselves your/yours themselves
Relative	who	whom	whose	whom

These cases show the function of nouns and pronouns in a sentence.

- In writing, the **speaking voice** from the author is called the *first person*. It is from the *I* or *we* perspective. The *second person* is the person *spoken to*. It is *you* to whom we refer or write.

  The *third person* is the person who is *spoken about*. *He, she*, and *it* are the third person singular, and *they* is the third person plural.

- The possessive case refers to one-self.

  *example*s: "That's *my* book," *or* "The book is *mine*"; "That's *our* uniform," *or* "The uniform is *ours*."

  —The reflexive case needs a subject, noun, or pronoun to precede it.

   *example*s: "It will be cleaned, even if *I* have to do it *myself*," *or* "*We* can do it all *ourselves*," and "Mother will cook it *herself*."

  —Pronouns can also be classified in other ways besides the chart above, the four Cases of Pronouns. Here are four other classifications by which pronouns may be grouped.

  —Indefinite: *one, any, anyone, each, either, somebody, someone, all, every*

  —Demonstrative: *this, that, these, those*

  —Interrogative: *who, which, what* (beginning a question)

Grammar, Usage, and Mechanics

Pronoun Practice

A. Write a pronoun to take the place of the word or words in each rectangle.

John F. Kennedy	abolitionists	contortionist	all the things you show me in your hands
your rival school	the things in your backpack	Madame Curie	the person doing this assignment
the author's royalties	photon	our competition	every object owned by your neighbors
your family	telemarketer (unknown sex)	all things on this Earth	all the boxes in a warehouse

B. Fill in the blanks with appropriate pronouns.

1. The child replied, "I can do it all by _____."

2. Sherry got the phone numbers of two boys at school. _____ wanted to go out with one of _____ Saturday night, but she wasn't sure _____ one to ask. So, she asked a neighbor to help. "_____ should I ask to go out with _____ this Saturday?" _____ asked _____ neighbor.

3. Mr. Jones stepped on the scale at the doctor's office. _____ read 225 pounds. Mr. Jones could not believe _____ eyes. "_____ guess I've gained a few too many. This body of _____ isn't growing any taller any more, is it? It's just a lot wider. It's _____ wife's rich cooking. What can _____ do?"
   The doctor replied, "_____ are going to have to lose this weight by dieting and exercising. _____ can do it for you. You'll have to do it _____."

4. It was late at night. _____ family stayed up to watch a movie. Suddenly there was a knock at the door. Dad called out, "_____ is it?" _____ answered; there wasn't a single sound. _____ didn't think much of _____ until the same thing happened again a few minutes later. _____ could it be bothering _____ this late at night, _____ wondered. _____ was really scaring _____ now. After the third knock, in about twenty minutes, _____ dad yelled out, "_____ have just called the police! _____ are on the way, right now!" _____ it was must have left right then because he or she never bothered _____ again.

Grammar, Usage, and Mechanics

Proper Pronoun Usage

Here is additional information to help understand the cases of pronouns and how to use them. Use this page together with page 26.

The **nominative** or **subjective case** is used when the writer is referring to the subject of a verb. The examples below will replace the names in each sentence with the appropriate nominative form.

example: Rebecca, Ashley, Sammy, David, and I swam.
nominative change: We swam.
example: My son Benny is cute.
nominative change: He is cute.
example: The writer of this book is tired of typing.
nominative change: I am tired of typing.

The nominative case should also be used after the words *as* and *than*. The following examples show how this is done.

example: Jason does his homework faster than the writer does.
nominative change: He does his homework faster that I do.
example: Michaela is as fast a runner as Tatiana and Maria are.
nominative change: She is as fast a runner as they are.

Also use the nominative case with the word *who* when it is referring to *he* or *she* (a subject pronoun).

example: Who is coming to the party? (In other words, someone is asking for the names of the people — the he's and she's — attending the party.)
example: May I say who is calling? (In other words, someone is asking, "May I say he or she is calling?")

In addition, use the nominative case after the conjunction *and*. See the following example.

example: Shawn and the writer of this book went out for ice cream.
nominative change: He and I went out for ice cream.

Lastly, use the nominative case after forms of the verb *to be*, such as the following: *is, are, was, were*, and *have been*.

example: It was the writer of this book who ate the chocolate cookie.
nominative change: It was I.
example: I thought it was Heather.
nominative change: I thought it was she.
example: It wasn't Karianne, Ethan, Jeremy, or I.
nominative change: It wasn't we.
example: Since that cookie was a gift, I would not want to be the girl who ate it!
nominative change: Since that cookie was a gift, I would not want to be she.

Proper Pronoun Usage (cont.)

Use the **possessive case** when the writer is referring to a noun or pronoun preceding a gerund (a word derived from a verb, ending in -ing, that is unable to stand as the main verb in a sentence).

examples: What is the reason for his losing the ticket?

He is annoyed by their keeping the secret.

In the possessive case use *which* to refer to impersonal antecedents and use *whose* to refer to situations where the phrase *of which* would sound awkward.

examples: On our drive through the country, we saw a barn whose roof was caving in.

The billy goat's attack on the other goats, which was very difficult to watch, was upsetting to me.

The **objective case** is used when the writer is referring to the object of a verb, a verbal, or a preposition (a word used to relate a noun or a pronoun to some other word in a sentence, such as *in, through, during, of,* and *with*). The following examples replace words with the appropriate objective pronouns.

example: I met Jordan.

objective change: I met him.

example: Visiting my brother's family was a frustrating experience.

objective change: Visiting them was a frustrating experience.

Use the objective case after the conjunction *and*, as in the following examples.

example: Mom found Jack doing his homework and me doing my homework.

objective change: Mom found him and me doing our homework.

example: I swam with Kenny and Aly.

objective change: I swam with him and her.

example: The team captain needs to choose between Brianna and the writer of this book.

objective change: The team captain needs to choose between her and me.

(**Note:** The correct form in the last sentence is not "her and I." It does not make sense to say, ". . . captain needs to choose . . . I." If you are not sure which form to use in confusing sentences such as these, try a test on them. Temporarily cross out the interrupting words as in the last example. You will immediately know what does and does not make sense.)

Also use the objective case with the word *whom*, which is actually referring to *him* or *her*.

example: To whom do you wish to speak?

This sentence is asking, "Do you wish to speak to him or her?" Using proper English, you would answer, "This is he/she," if the caller wishes to speak to you. In this instance, you are saying, "He/she is speaking." You wouldn't say," This is him/her," because that would be the same as saying, "Him/her is speaking."

Grammar, Usage, and Mechanics

Crazy Cases

Rewrite the following sentences to correct the pronoun errors. An example has been done for you.

example: She and me went to the store.
revision: She and I went to the store.

1. Their family has lived there longer than us. _____

2. It was her who was elected prom queen. _____

3. When we heard the tap on the window, we knew it was him. _____

4. We found John and she at the park. _____

5. Who do you wish to replace, he or I? _____

6. Our rude neighbors reported he as well as I to the police for something that wasn't even done by we. _____

7. Yours is the car of which front end is parked on the property of us. _____

8. You and them were in the play we saw last night. _____

9. Janie was the girl for who all the seventh and eighth grade boys voted. _____

10. In the distance the man resembled my grandfather. Shocked, I just stared, almost thinking it was him. _____

Verbs

Verbs are words that indicate action. Their forms tell what is being done, by whom, and—if there is an object—to what or whom. They also tell when something is happening, will happen, or did happen. There are several types of verbs.

Often, verbs are defined as **action verbs** or **non-action verbs**. Action verbs tell what the subject of a sentence does.

examples: itch, glorify, glimmer, tease, fret, wrestle, listen, participate, murmur

Non-action verbs express a state of being rather than doing. They join the subject of a sentence with another word or phrase by telling what the subject has or does. For example, if we say Lorenzo has a laughing parrot, the non-action verb is *has*.

examples: has, had, have, is, are, was, were, am, been, can, will

Verbs combine with **auxiliaries**, which are verb forms used with the main verb to form a verb phrase. Auxiliaries are commonly found in two groups, the first of which is used to indicate tense and voice. This group includes the following: *shall, will,* and the forms of *be, have,* and *do* (for example, *shall nap, will nap, has napped, had napped, does nap, is napping, was napping*). The second group, **modal auxiliaries**, includes the following: *can, could, may, might, must, ought, should,* and *would.* These are used to indicate ability, permission, obligation, and the like (for example, *can nap, could nap, may nap, might nap, must nap, ought to nap, should nap, would nap*).

Verbs may also be classified as **transitive**, meaning that they require an object (for example, "He made spaghetti.") or **intransitive**, not requiring an object (for example, "They danced."). Many verbs can function as both (for example, "The wind blew," and "She blew her nose.").

Linking verbs show a relation between a subject of a sentence and a complement. They refer to the five senses. The principle linking verbs are as follows: *be, become, appear,* and *seem.*

examples: You *seem* a little green around the gills. Have you *become* ill? You *appear* to have lost the color in your face. You could *be* feverish.

Last but not least, verbs are critical to voice. They can command in the **imperative** voice. (*Listen* to your teacher.) And, they can set a mood in the **subjunctive** voice. (*If I were* in Hawaii right now, I'd be so happy.)

Here are some final important notes about the subjunctive.

    a. It is used mostly for hypothetical situations (things that have not happened or are not likely to happen).

       example: If I were taller, I'd be a basketball player.

    b. It can also express a need for urgency.

       example: It is essential that this medicine *be tested* thoroughly before it is given to humans.

Grammar, Usage, and Mechanics

Verb Curb

Read each set of rhyming words. Determine which are and which are not verbs. Circle the verbs in each set. (The use of a dictionary is advised.)

1. yearn   turn   spurn   urn   earn   learn   burn
   adjourn   churn

2. daze   amaze   days   haze   bays   cays   faze
   graze   gaze   jays   laze   maze   raise   stays

3. gasp   clasp   grasp   asp   hasp   rasp

4. clever   ever   whomever   never   lever   sever

5. leave   cleave   believe   grieve   heave   receive   Steve
   retrieve   weave   achieve

6. dour   devour   bower   tower   flour   cower   flower
   hour   our   power   sour   dower

7. share   chair   stair   stare   affair   éclair   hair
   bare   bear   care   dare   declare   glare   fair
   fare   lair   mare   pear   rare   tear   wear
   underwear   spare   flair   ensnare   Delaware   flare

Challenge

Make a list of your own rhyming verbs for numbers 8–10. Trade your paper and have a classmate find and circle the verbs.

8.

9.

10.

Grammar, Usage, and Mechanics

Verbacious Sentences

Circle the verb in each sentence. Below the sentence, write as many other verbs as you can think of that might make a better sentence. You may use a thesaurus for help.

1. He compiled a list of documents. _____

2. The historical monument has deteriorated in the past ten years.

3. Once outside the prison walls, the inmate indulged in a wonderful meal. _____

4. The child scampered through the yard.

5. The student has been inspired by the guest speaker.

6. The skunk's odor saturated his clothes. _____

7. We prohibit the use of drugs in school. _____

8. The king lauded his knights for their valor. _____

9. They subverted their enemies. _____

10. The candidate for presidency defeated his opponent in the debate. _____

Grammar, Usage, and Mechanics

Adjectives and Adverbs

Adjectives are words used to describe nouns and pronouns. They are usually placed either immediately before or after the noun they modify. They can reveal what kind (*poor* report or *noteworthy* essay), how many (*several* awards or *three* boys), or which one (*furthest* car or *this* pen). There are different types of adjectives. They include *articles, common adjectives, demonstrative, indefinite,* and *possessive.*

Articles describe nouns and pronouns in an indefinite way. There are just three articles. They are *a, an,* and *the.*

Common adjectives describe the subject in a definite way. They answer the questions "What kind?" and "How many?"
   examples: tender, lukewarm, thirteen, turquoise, exhausted, translucent

Proper adjectives are made from proper nouns and are always capitalized. They answer the question "What kind?"
   examples: Irish, Native American, Elizabethan, Japanese

Demonstrative adjectives point out things. They answer the question "Which one(s)?"
   examples: this, that, these, those

Indefinite adjectives give an approximate amount or number.
   examples: some, many, more, less, fewer

Possessive adjectives show belonging.
   examples: my, his, her, their

Adverbs describe verbs, adjectives, and other adverbs.
   example of verb description: He ran *swiftly* to win the race.
   example of adjective description: The *astoundingly* beautiful sunset awed us.
   example of adverb description: The school year went *surprisingly* well.

   —Adverbs tell the extent of something.
      example: I am *very* exhausted. I worked *too* hard today.

   —Adverbs tell when or where something happens.
      example: *Tomorrow* I will clean my room and put my desk *here* in the corner.

   —Adverbs tell how and how often something happens.
      example: She *always* shares *generously* with everyone.

   —Adverbs often end with the letters *-ly*, but not always, as you can see from the examples above. Also, some words that end in *-ly* are not adverbs, such as *lovely* and *fly*.

Adjectives and Adverbs (cont.)

Comparative and Superlative

Adjectives and adverbs have distinctive forms in the **comparative** and **superlative** classifications. In the comparative form, certain words end with *-er* or are joined by the word *more* to express a greater degree or to make a comparison.

examples: sadder, more beautiful, more quickly

Superlatives, formed by adding *–est* or by putting *most* before the positive form indicates the greatest degree, quality, or quantity among a group of people or things.

example: saddest, most beautiful, quickest

Note that when comparing two things, one of them cannot be "the most." Two items may only take the comparative form.

There are a few rules that dictate when to use the words *more* or *most* and the endings *-er* and *-est*. The rules are dependent on the amount of syllables the adjective or adverb has. For instance, when a word has only one syllable like *nice* or *fat*, it can usually form the comparative or superlative with *-er* and *-est*, becoming *nicer*, *nicest*, *fatter*, and *fattest*. When an adjective has two syllables, it can take variant forms, such as *fancier, more fancy, craziest,* and *most crazy*. Adjectives and adverbs that have three or more syllables always form the comparative and superlative by using *more* and *most*, as in *more wonderful* and *most regretfully*.

Some adjectives and adverbs have irregular forms. They can perform just like comparatives and superlatives in that they express something to a greater degree and make comparisons between things, but they retain their irregular forms. Examples of such words are *good, better, best, badly, worse,* and *worst*.

Lastly, some adjectives and adverbs cannot logically be compared because their meanings are absolute. These words are *unique, empty, dead, perfect*, and *round*. One circle cannot be more round than another, and one dead bug on the windshield cannot be deader than another. Therefore, these words do not fit the patterns for superlative and comparative forms described previously.

Grammar, Usage, and Mechanics

A nonfiction reading & writing program • A nonfiction reading & writing program

This Is More Interesting!

The sentences below are uninteresting. Your job is to rewrite each sentence, adding or changing the adjectives and adverbs to make the sentences interesting for the reader.

1. Merlin, the magician, designed many neat tricks.
   _____

2. The stuffy queen is a snob.
   _____

3. When they saw the creature's shadow, the green frogs hopped into the pond.
   _____

4. The large man shouted his battle cry.
   _____

5. The inventor presented his contraption.
   _____

6. The insect buzzed loudly in my ear.
   _____

7. The captors danced wildly around the captive.
   _____

8. The laborer was very hot.
   _____

9. The man stumbled and fell.
   _____

10. The meat is quickly spoiling.
    _____

Grammar, Usage, and Mechanics

A nonfiction reading & writing program • A nonfiction reading & writing program

Descriptive Quilt

For this activity, you will need colored pencils and page 34 as a reference. Color the spaces with proper adjectives purple, indefinite adjectives yellow, possessive adjectives red, demonstrative adjectives green, common adjectives blue, and adverbs orange. Leave uncolored everything else.

theirs / immobile (Russian)	approximately / inferior (elegant)	eventually / several (discord)	colossal / his (Renaissance)
aperture / aviation (various, ours)	that / discourage (elegant, moody)	vigorous / interfering (acne)	ambush / those (hers, major)
totally / well	this / more (Victorian, my)	shady / commendable (quarrel)	populace / these (cynical)	less / always (Panamanian, its)	gradually
yours / concealed (Mongolian)	mobility / very (additional)	bicycle / too (further)	ludicrous / their (Communist)

©Teacher Created Materials, Inc.

Grammar, Usage, and Mechanics

Adjective and Adverb Use

Use colored pen or pencil in the following sentences to correct the errors in adjective and adverb use.

1. Adam is the most tallest of the two boys.

2. The Rose Parade floats rolled majestic down the street.

3. He is the lazy boy I've ever met.

4. America cars always break down.

5. The play is tragically.

6. The counselor gave the arguable couple a disapproved look.

7. The wildly roller coaster dips and turns in a thrill ride.

8. The wreck wasn't near as bad as it could have been if the driver had not been driving so responsible.

9. He looked suspicious at me!

10. A teacher works considerable harder than many other professions for lesser pay.

11. She worked hasty on her chores so she could finish and visit a sicker friend.

12. The outdated school campus irritated greatly the students severely.

13. I came upon quite a noisily scene as I walked down the street: two dogs barking loud at a scare cat up a tree.

14. The construction worker exhausted himself too much in the hot sun and passed out from the extremely heat.

15. "Either clean these room, young man, or spend the next week without no television!" his mother yelled irate.

Grammar, Usage, and Mechanics

Prepositions, Conjunctions, and Interjections

Prepositions are words that relate a noun or a pronoun to another word in a sentence. They show physical relationships between things in a sentence.

example: The goat is *in* my washroom.

The preposition *in* shows the relationship between *goat* and *washroom*. The statement, "The goat is now *on* my dryer," uses *on* to explain the relation between *goat* and *dryer*. *To* does the same in the following sentence: "I grabbed him by the horns, and I am taking him back *to* the goat yard."

The preposition and its object form a **prepositional phrase.** The prepositional phrases in the examples above are as follows.

examples: ". . . in (*preposition*) my washroom (*object*)."
". . . on (*preposition*) my dryer (*object*)."
". . . to (*preposition*) the goat yard (*object*)."

(The careful reader will likewise note that "by the horns" is also a prepositional phrase.)

Common prepositions include the following: *about, above, across, after, against, among, around, at, before, beside, beyond, between, by, down, during, except, for, from, in, into, near, of, off, on, over, through, to, toward, under, until, up,* and *with*.

Conjunctions join words, phrases, or clauses, showing the relationship between the sentence parts they connect. **Coordinating conjunctions** have the function of joining words, phrases, or clauses of equal grammatical rank, as follows:

example of joined words: She planted flowers *and* trees.
example of joined phrases: Search in the refrigerator *or* on top of the pantry.
example of joined clauses: We wanted to stay, *but* we were too tired.

Correlative conjunctions are seen in pairs: *either/or, neither/nor, both/and,* and *not only/but also*.

examples: *Neither* peanut butter *nor* jelly go well with fried pickles.
We are going to *both* the lake *and* the sea.
I asked *not only* for ketchup *but also* for hot sauce.

Subordinating conjunctions introduce clauses and join them to main clauses. Here are some of the most commonly used subordinating conjunctions: *because, if, since, when,* and *where*. Below is an example of how they work.

*example*s: The river was rising higher *because* the dam had a leak.
If it continues to rise any higher, we shall have to evacuate.

Interjections are exclamatory words that express emotion. They have no grammatical relation to other words in a sentence. When writing interjections, follow mild ones with a comma and stronger ones with an exclamation point. Here are some examples for each.

examples: *Oh my*, I think you need a bath.
Yes, I'd love to go.
Wow! Is that for me?
Ugh! This is driving me crazy!

Grammar, Usage, and Mechanics

Construction Zone

Construct sentences to fit each formula described below. Consider being humorous or writing vivid descriptions to add interest to your written work.

1. Adjective + noun + verb + adverb.

   _____

2. Three adjectives + noun + verb + adverb + prepositional phrase.

   _____

3. Pronoun + verb + adverb + prepositional phrase + conjunction + verb + noun.

   _____

4. Adverb + noun + verb + prepositional phrase.

   _____

5. Interjection + pronoun + verb + adverb + prepositional phrase + conjunction + adjective + noun + verb.

   _____

   _____

6. Pronoun + conjunction + pronoun + verb + adverb + noun + preposition + adjective + noun.

   _____

   _____

7. Two adjectives + noun + conjunction + adjective + plural noun + verb + adverb + preposition + adjective + plural noun.

   _____

   _____

8. Correlative conjunctions (used where needed) + noun + adjective + noun + verb + adverb + preposition + adjective + noun.

   _____

Grammar, Usage, and Mechanics

A nonfiction reading & writing program • A nonfiction reading & writing program

Sort 'Em

Write each word below in the correct column on the chart.

Verbs	Nouns	Adjectives	Adverbs

Conjunctions	Interjections	Pronouns	Prepositions

you	tessellation	selfishly	herself
tonight	credibly	myself	innocuous
so	revere	during	impoverish
reverent	in	yet	Cubans
and	oops	mine	or
beside	innocent	insubordinate	yuck
through	integrity	nevermore	wow
for	intimidate	but	panacea
parry	I	it	from
dross	because	nor	

©Teacher Created Materials, Inc.

Grammar, Usage, and Mechanics

Spelling Helps

The English language has taken its many forms from several other languages, so spelling rules are not quite uniform. Keep in mind that there are always exceptions to the rules, but the rules can be helpful in spelling the majority of words correctly. You will just have to memorize the spellings of the irregular words or check them in a dictionary or computer spell-check. Here are several spelling rules to aid in correct spelling.

1. Write *i* before *e*, except after *c*, or when sounding like *long a* as in *neighbor* and *weigh*.
   i before e examples: brief, yield
   ei after c examples: ceiling, receive
   long a examples: vein, sleigh
   exceptions to the i before e rule: their, height, neither, foreign, weird, either, seize, leisure
   exceptions to the ei after c rule: ancient, science, financier, species

2. Drop the final *e* before a suffix *beginning with a vowel* because the purpose of that final *e* in the root word is to make the first vowel sound long. When you drop the *e*, the suffix replaces it and has the same impact on the first vowel sound of the root word.
   examples: slide + ing = sliding, like + ed = liked

3. Keep the final *e* before a suffix beginning with a vowel to retain the soft sound of *c* or *g*.
   examples: notice + able = noticeable, change + able = changeable

4. Drop the final *e* in a word with a soft *c* or *g* only when a suffix begins with *i* or *e*.
   examples: age + ing = aging, change + ed = changed

5. Do not drop the final *e* before a suffix beginning with a consonant because the final *e* is needed to retain the long vowel sound in the root word.
   examples: like + ness = likeness, defense + less = defenseless

6. Rule exception: drop the *e* in short words when you add *–ly* and *–ful*.
   examples: true + ly = truly, awe + ful = awful

7. Change the *ie* ending of words to a *y* before adding *–ing*.
   examples: die + ing = dying, untie + ing = untying

8. The final *y* is changed to *i* before a suffix (starting with any letter other than *i*) is added.
   examples: happy + ness = happiness, pretty + er = prettier, vary + ous = various

9. If a root word ends in *y* preceded by a vowel, usually keep the *y* before adding any suffix.
   examples: joy + ful = joyful, survey + or = surveyor
   exceptions: pay + ed = paid, day + ly = daily

Grammar, Usage, and Mechanics

Now That Your Head Is Spinning, Spell It

Spell each of the following words correctly and explain what spelling rule applies from page 42.

1. arrange + ment = _____ Rule # _____
2. please + ure = _____ Rule # _____
3. convey + ance = _____ Rule # _____
4. untie + ing = _____ Rule # _____
5. replace + ment = _____ Rule # _____
6. preserve + ing = _____ Rule # _____
7. cranky + ness = _____ Rule # _____
8. pursue + ing = _____ Rule # _____
9. state + ment = _____ Rule # _____
10. generalize + ed = _____ Rule # _____
11. renounce + ing = _____ Rule # _____
12. due + ly = _____ Rule # _____
13. associate + ion = _____ Rule # _____
14. busy + ness = _____ Rule # _____
15. change + able = _____ Rule # _____
16. change + ing = _____ Rule # _____
17. conceive + able = _____ Rule # _____
18. eighty + eth = _____ Rule # _____
19. courage + ous = _____ Rule # _____
20. Which is the correct spelling in each pair? Circle it.

variety . . . . vareity
anxiety . . . . anxiety
deciet . . . . deceit
fiend . . . . feind
impatient . . . . . impateint
skien . . . . skein
reciept . . . . receipt

percieve . . . . . . perceive
priest . . . . preist
beseige . . . . besiege
neighbor . . . . . nieghbor
foriegn . . . . foreign
financier . . . . . financeir
siezure . . . . seizure

©Teacher Created Materials, Inc.   #3570 Grammar, Usage, and Mechanics

Grammar, Usage, and Mechanics

More Spelling Rules: Who Made Up This Stuff?

Here are some more important spelling rules to learn and use. Do your best to review them in your mind so that you can use them when you need a word you do not know how to spell. Keep in mind, however, that there are always exceptions to the rules.

1. Add *s* to singular nouns or verbs unless they do not sound smooth.
    examples: sculptures, memorials, catastrophes, communicates

2. Add *–es* to nouns ending in *ch, sh, x, ss, z,* and *o* (preceded by a consonant).
    examples: pitches, dishes, taxes, masses, buzzes, potatoes

3. Add *–ves* to plural nouns that end in *f* or *fe*.
    examples: knives, calves, wolves, wives

4. Words that end with a vowel preceding an *o* form the plural by adding *s*.
    examples: stereos, radios, shampoos

5. Double a consonant (with the exception of *w, y, s,* or *x*) in a one-syllable, short vowel word when adding a suffix beginning with a vowel. This keeps the sound of the preceding vowel short.
    examples: hopping, swimmer, slippage, quizzing

    (Note: Since the letters *qu* always go together, the *u* is not considered the first vowel.)

Do you know why *keeping* is not spelled *keepping*, why *boxes* is not spelled *boxxes*, and why *sadness* is not spelled *saddness*? Think about the rules listed above. Which ones apply?

Keeping has a long vowel sound. There is no need to double the *p*. The only reason to do so would be to keep the first vowel sound short when a suffix starting with a vowel is added. *Boxes*, on the other hand, does have a short first vowel sound. However, it is one of those exceptions to the rules. Reread what is written inside of the parentheses in rule # 5. *Sadness* also has a short first vowel sound, but it is not an exception to the rule. Reread rule #5. It is referring only to short vowel words that add a suffix beginning with a vowel (not with a consonant, as in *–ness*.)

Grammar, Usage, and Mechanics

More Spelling Rules: Who Made Up This Stuff? (cont.)

6. When adding a suffix, double the final consonant in a multi-syllable word if it ends with a *single consonant* (not *x*) preceded by a *single vowel* and the accent falls on the last syllable.

   examples: beginning, omitted, omission, preferred, admitting, admission, forbidden

   Refer to this as the *last-syllable* rule. Sometimes the accent switches places, as in the word *cancel*. However, *canceled*, *canceler*, and *canceling* do not have the double *ll* because the accent is in the front of the word. When you add *-ation* to the end of the word, however, the accent switches to the back of the root word and the result is *cancellation*.

   Therefore, you can summarize that this rule is based on *accent placement*. As the accent shifts, spellings must reflect a change in emphasis in words such as *reference*, *preferable*, *difference*, *worshiper*, *traveling*, and *profiting*. Here the accent is in the first part of the word, so the final consonant of the base word is not doubled.

7. When a base word begins with the same letter with which a prefix ends, keep both letters when adding that prefix.

   examples: dissatisfy, unneeded, deemphasis

8. If the base word ends with the same letter with which a suffix begins, *keep both letters*. However, do not keep more than two of the same letter.

   examples: suddenness, carefully, dully

9. Use hyphens to add *–less* and *–like* to words ending in double *ll*.

   example: cell-like, shell-less

To help avoid misspellings, do the following:

- Learn the spelling rules.

- Remember there are always exceptions, so check a dictionary.

- Memorize by breaking troublesome words into syllables, so small parts can be learned before the whole.

- Spell it aloud or on paper without looking at the correctly spelled word, and then check your spelling.

- Review steps #3 and #4 several times until you are able to spell the word correctly each time.

Grammar, Usage, and Mechanics

Spell It ~~Write~~ Right

Rewrite each sentence by spelling the misspelled words correctly. You will need additional paper.

1. I beleive it's admireable to be peacful during times of unecessary ungovernnable agitateion.

2. The managment has busyed itself in presuading the corporation to raise the salarys of the secretarys.

3. I am disatisfyed with the outcome of my recent surgerys; the scars are realy noticable. I feel the doctors decieved me by assureing me there would be no disfigurment.

4. She admited that she truly benefitted from the jugement that accidentaly frede her from all liabilitys in the civil case.

5. The ambituous young executiv is also an aspireing politition.

6. The little actress has become quite ostentatous, and it's all because her unscruppulous mother sees to it that her daughter gets whatever roles she finds desireable at any cost.

7. The locatetion of the churchs the missionarys are visiting is confuseing. The dirt roades are not servicable, being holey and unstable. The surounding area is steep and mountainus, seemingly unsuiteable for any buildings besides hutts. Perplexd, the emissarys are seeking the asisstance of the locale inhabitantes to find the correct way to the establishmants.

8. The preschoollers in our school were acting very crankey one day. I was asisting in there room, and they were about to drive me crazy. I mean it! At lunchtime, one little tot complaned histericaly that he wanted a carrot stick, not a carrot. What's the diffrence? Then when we were singing, another youngstere was so unruley; he kept pulling people's hair, moving all over when he should have been in one place, and screechhing rather than singing. I was despairring of ever getting through that classs. When it was finaly over the teacher aproached me and comennded me for my patience. I guess I managged a lot better than I had previusly thought.

Grammar, Usage, and Mechanics

A nonfiction reading & writing program • A nonfiction reading & writing program

Agreement

Your job is to train yourself to use Standard English in your writing. Standard English is the spoken and written language of educated people, such as professionals, businessmen and women, and educators. It is also the langauge of the law, journalism, and most literature.

Training to become competent in the use of Standard English is hard work—it takes a lot of practice. Learn from your mistakes by paying attention to how you have erred and how you can improve. Competence in its use is necessary to taking part in the mainstream of business, politics, and even culture.

Agreement is the grammatical relationship between words in certain forms. Verbs agree with their subjects in number and in person. In *he laughs*, for example, both *he* and *laughs* are singular and written in the third person. Pronouns agree with their antecedents in person, number, and gender. In the sentence, *she ate her pizza*, *she* and *her* are third person and feminine. Demonstrative adjectives match the nouns they modify in number.

   example: *This man is* buying a ticket right now. *Those men are waiting* in line to buy *theirs* next.

Below are some helpful suggestions to use while writing to increase sentence clarity and effectiveness.

1. Make verbs agree in number with their subjects. Do not let words that intervene between subjects and verbs confuse you. Find the subject and make sure the verb agrees with it.

   example: The first three *scenes* of the play *were* boring.

   In this sentence, the subject is the word *scenes*. The verb *were* agrees with it, not with the nearest noun, *play*.

   faulty example: Tom, together with all of his teammates, were dousing the coach with water.
   correct revision: Tom, together with all of his teammates, was dousing the coach with water.

   To correctly show agreement in this sentence, realize that the subject, *Tom* (not *teammates*), agrees with the verb, *was dousing*.

2. Use a singular pronoun to refer to antecedents such as the following: *person, man, woman, one, any, anyone, anybody, someone, someone, each, every, everybody, everyone, either,* and *neither*.

   examples: *Everyone* sat in *his* seat. *Neither* of the teachers wanted to fail *anyone* of *his* (or *her*) students.

   exception: When *each* is written after the plural subject, the verb form is not affected. Both of the following sentences are written correctly. A. The pig and goat each *has its* own cage. B. The pig and goat each *have their* own cages.

Grammar, Usage, and Mechanics

Agreement (cont.)

3. Use a plural verb when subjects are joined by *and*.

   example: Her dog and cat *are* fighting.

   The exception is that you should use a singular verb when the compound subject refers to the same person or thing.

   example: My doctor and friend *has* come to console me. (*Doctor* and *friend*, in this sentence, refer to the same person.)

4. Singular subjects joined by *either/or* or *neither/nor* use a singular verb unless the subjects differ in number and in person. If so, the verb will agree with the closest subject.

   examples: Either the doctor or the nurse *was* to have signed your papers.

   Neither the teacher nor the skating students *were* aware of the banana peel on the ground.

   Neither the skating students nor the teacher *was* aware of the banana peel on the ground.

5. When a verb comes before the subject of a sentence, make them agree with one another.

   examples: There *are* only a bed set and a toy box left at the garage sale.

   There *are* many old photographs in the attic.

6. When using the pronouns *who*, *which*, and *that*, use a singular verb when the antecedent is singular and a plural verb when the antecedent is plural.

   example: She is the only one on the staff *who* is going to the conference.

7. Use a singular verb with collective nouns (for example, *news*, *majority*, and *community*), because each is considered a unit.

   examples: Mathematics *is* my hardest subject.

   The management *was* investigating the problem.

   Twenty dollars *is* too expensive for that video.

   Here is the exception. If a group or quantity is regarded as individuals or parts (not a unit), use a plural verb.

   example: Many of the council *were* sick.

8. A linking verb needs to agree with its subject, not its complement (a word, excluding an adjective or adverb, which helps complete the meaning of the verb, such as the direct or indirect object).

   example: Punctuality problems *were* the reason for his termination.

   You can also change the word placement in this sentence and it will alter the linking verb.

   example: The reason for his termination *was* punctuality problems.

Grammar, Usage, and Mechanics

To Agree or Not To Agree

Read each sentence. Determine if it is written correctly. If so, write "OK" before the sentence. If incorrect, write the number of the applicable rule (pages 47 and 48) in the space before the sentence. Then revise the sentence.

1. The timing of the school assemblies was an annoyance to several of the teachers.

2. There is a few bouncing balls and jump ropes left in the ball room.

3. The first ten customers was to receive a gift certificate.

4. The majority are angry about the mayor's decision.

5. Everyone in my family, including my dog, has blue eyes.

6. The point of the conversation were differences between girls and boys and how to get along with one another.

7. In the garage there is my dad's hot rods.

8. Neither the children nor the babysitter were to eat the popsicles in the freezer.

9. The chewy candies in my candy bag are the only ones left that gets stuck in my teeth.

10. Every policeman and fireman came to make their appearances at the community cook-off.

Grammar, Usage, and Mechanics

Writing It Right

Use the charts below to help you know when to use each form of the following verbs.

Chart A

Use when referring to one person or thing.	Use when referring to more than one person or thing.
there is/is there	there are/are there
is/isn't	are/aren't
was/wasn't	were/weren't
had/has	have

Chart B

Use without the help of a helping verb.	Use with a helping verb: *had, has, have, is, are, was, were.*
saw	seen
did	done
went	gone
took	taken
came	come
ran	run (past tense)
broke	broken

Fill in each blank with a verb from Chart A or B.

1. When the bus overturned in the ditch, it was later learned that the occupants had _____ many bones.

2. Upon interviewing a witness of the accident, the public ascertained that there _____ no one else at the scene to help at the time.

3. The witness _____ what he could to help, but it _____ enough. There _____ too many injured people and it would have _____ him all day to free everyone from the wreckage and rubble.

4. Finally someone _____ the wreck and _____ to help. The work would have been exhausting for the two "good Samaritans" if a trucker hadn't also _____ the crash and _____ for help.

5. The emergency response team arrived soon after and _____ to work freeing the rest of the crash victims.

#3570 Grammar, Usage, and Mechanics ©Teacher Created Materials, Inc.

Grammar, Usage, and Mechanics

Irregular Plurals

1. When forming a plural for a proper noun, add *s* if the noun does not already end in *s*. Add *-es* if it does. Do not change a *v* or *y* ending to an *f* or *i*.

    *example*s: The Alexander family becomes the Alexanders.
    The Jones family becomes the Joneses.
    The Wolf family becomes the Wolfs.
    The Perry family becomes the Perrys.
    The McKenzie family becomes the McKenzies.

2. Irregular plural nouns do not have *s* or *-es* added to their endings. Some remain unchanged, regardless of whether they are singular or plural. Others have altogether different endings. Below is a partial list of those nouns that remain unchanged whether they are singular or plural.

    - fish
    - moose
    - deer
    - sheep
    - species
    - corps
    - rendezvous
    - salmon

These irregular plurals have altogether different endings than their singular counterparts.

Singular	Plural
mouse	mice
ox	oxen
goose	geese
foot	feet
tooth	teeth
person	people
woman	women
man	men
child	children
louse	lice
alumnus	alumni
analysis	analyses
basis	bases
hypothesis	hypotheses
phenomenon	phenomena
memorandum	memoranda
crisis	crises

Irregular Plurals (cont.)

3. Some compound words are simply made plural by adding *s*. Others are formed and act like irregular plurals. Below is a partial list of them.

Singular	Plural
passerby	passersby
forefoot	forefeet
grandchild	grandchildren
catfish	catfishes
goldfish	goldfish
homework	homework
workman	workmen

   (**Note:** Change *man* to *men* with any compound word that uses *man* to refer to a person.)

4. When a compound word is hyphenated or consisting of separate words, make plural the main element of that word.
   examples: sisters-in-law, runners-up, attorneys-general
   exceptions: time-outs, hang-ups

5. When the main element of the compound word phrase is possessive, make the other word in the phrase plural.
   examples: traveler's checks, rabbit's feet

6. If the hyphenated compound word is plural and possessive, follow the above rules and simply add *s*.
   examples: mothers-in-law's recipes, passers-by's right of way

Grammar, Usage, and Mechanics

A nonfiction reading & writing program • A nonfiction reading & writing program

That's Some Story!

What a mess! Correct the mistakes in the use of singular and plural words in this paragraph, using colored pencil or pen to do so.

> The alumnis of O'Grady High School—they call themselves the O'Gradies Graduates—went on several wildlife seeing fieldtrips this past summer. Many persons participated. Three members of the Humphrieses family also attended. (Mr. Humphries is our schoolses principal, by the ways.) During their many rendezvouses, they enjoyed seeing salmon's runs, a fish hatchery, and mixed varieties of fishes, wild mooses, deers, and geeses.
>
> On one such trip, a few of the womans and their childs wandered off in search of an outhouse. They witnessed a strange phenomena. Some mouses were seen baring their tooths at one another. The woman talked amongst themselves about the oddity of such behavior and made an analyses: the creatures must have simply been afraid of the passer-byers and were, in all probability, reacting to them.

Challenge

Can you create a mess like the one above? (It may be tough now that you have become so educated!) How often are you given an assignment that is supposed to have mistakes? The catch is that you may only make errors in the use of irregular singular and plural words. So, go ahead and write a short story such as the one above. When you have finished, trade with a classmate and let him or her correct your mistakes.

Grammar, Usage, and Mechanics

A nonfiction reading & writing program • A nonfiction reading & writing program

Blast From the Past

Now that you have had instruction in spelling applications, making plurals, and in the use of apostrophes, can you keep from getting confused? Choose one of the words in parentheses to complete each sentence below so that it is correct.

1. In their nursery, all of the _____ (baby's, babies, babies') bottles are sterilized.

2. There was an investigation into the loss of revenue within our business. I think my _____ (bosses', bosses's, boss's) new Porsche serves as a clue as to who may be guilty.

3. The emperors had a royal ball to help them find suitable _____ (empresses, empress's, empress') to marry.

4. A cowboy's job description is laborious: _____ (ropeing, roping, ropping), branding, rounding-up steers, and spending a majority of the time in the hot sun on an old dusty trail.

5. Contact lenses are often _____ (prefered, preferred, preffered) over _____ (glasses, glasses', glass's), which can be heavy and sometimes obstruct peripheral vision.

6. My dog is the _____ (happyest, happest, happiest) when he is _____ (burying, buriing, burrying) his bones.

7. The _____ (Mosses, Mosses', Moss's), our new neighbors, are reconstructing the former _____ (owner's, owners, owners's) home.

8. Dad has _____ (admited, admitted, addmited) that he keeps _____ (forgetting, forrgetting, forggeting) which brand of laundry detergent is mom's _____ (preffence, preference, preferrence).

9. The _____ (babie's, baby's, babys') _____ (blankets', blanket's, blankets) _____ (spots, spots', spot's) have _____ (spots, spots', spot's) on them too— _____ (its, its', it's) so filthy.

10. The _____ (Cook's, Cooks's, Cooks) are having a garage sale. We want to buy two _____ (radioes, radios, radio's), but Grandpa yells at us about the money we're spending and his voice _____ (echos, echoss, echoes) off the _____ (neighbor's, neighbors's, neighbors) house. I am so embarrassed!

Grammar, Usage, and Mechanics

Root Words

A **root word** is a kind of base to which **prefixes** and **suffixes** may be added. Root words often come from the Greek and Latin languages. Studying roots, prefixes, and suffixes can help you to understand many difficult words. For instance, if you know the root *mal*, which means *bad*, you can learn the meanings of the following words with greater ease:

*mal*ediction—to slander
*mal*evolent—exhibiting ill will or malice
*mal*formation—abnormal or irregular form
*mal*ignant—pathological growth that spreads
dis*mal*—causing gloom

Note that not every definition for words containing *mal* will have a meaning that involves *bad* in some way. Language has changed over time; therefore, so have the meanings of some root words. So, you cannot always rely on roots to give an exact meaning, but more often than not, they can be helpful.

Look up the following roots and write their meanings. Then list five words that contain each root and also give their definitions. Here is the outline for what you are to do. You will probably need to write on a separate sheet of paper in order to have enough room.

Root	Meaning	Five Words	Definitions of Words
bene		1. 2. 3. 4. 5.	1. 2. 3. 4. 5.
fer		1. 2. 3. 4. 5.	1. 2. 3. 4. 5.
micro		1. 2. 3. 4. 5.	1. 2. 3. 4. 5.
port		1. 2. 3. 4. 5.	1. 2. 3. 4. 5.
phobos		1. 2. 3. 4. 5.	1. 2. 3. 4. 5.

Grammar, Usage, and Mechanics

Prefixes First, Suffixes Last

A **prefix** is a word element attached to the front of a root word that changes or modifies the root's meaning. For instance, *kind* means *nice and generous*, whereas *unkind* means the opposite because of the added prefix. Here are fifteen of the most common prefixes and their meanings:

ab—from	*dis*—part	*pre*—before
ad—to	*en*—in	*pro*—in front of
be—by	*ex*—out	*re*—back
com—with	*in*—into	*sub*—under
de—from	*in*—not	*un*—not

A **suffix** is a word element attached to the end of a root word. It modifies the root's meaning as well. Suffixes may be **inflectional**, such as an *s* added to nouns to form plurals (books, cars, dogs) or *-ed* added to verbs to indicate past tense (played, jumped, climbed). They may also be **derivational**, which can change the root's part of speech. Here are some of the most common such suffixes and their meanings:

ful—capable of being	*able*—capable of being
some—state of being	*ness*—state of being
ity—state of being	*ish*—state of being
age—act or state of	*ly*—like, in manner
er—little, maker of	*less*—without
est—comparison	*ment*—state or quality
ise/ize—to make	*ship*—relationship
tion—state or condition	*tude*—state or condition
ure—act or process	*ward*—direction of

Grammar, Usage, and Mechanics

A nonfiction reading & writing program • A nonfiction reading & writing program

First and Last

Define each word. Then list its stem and meaning, its prefix and meaning, and its suffix and meaning. Finally, write each word in the appropriate blank on the next page so that it makes sense in the sentence. (Yes, you may use a dictionary!)

1. **disinclination**: _____
   - stem: _____ meaning: _____
   - prefix: _____ meaning: _____
   - suffix: _____ meaning: _____

2. **innumerable**: _____
   - stem: _____ meaning: _____
   - prefix: _____ meaning: _____
   - suffix: _____ meaning: _____

3. **unsympathetic**: _____
   - stem: _____ meaning: _____
   - prefix: _____ meaning: _____
   - suffix: _____ meaning: _____

4. **substandardized**: _____
   - stem: _____ meaning: _____
   - prefix: _____ meaning: _____
   - suffix: _____ meaning: _____

5. **impersonal**: _____
   - stem: _____ meaning: _____
   - prefix: _____ meaning: _____
   - suffix: _____ meaning: _____

6. **misrepresentation**: _____
   - stem: _____ meaning: _____
   - prefix: _____ meaning: _____
   - suffix: _____ meaning: _____

7. **inconvenience**: _____
   - stem: _____ meaning: _____
   - prefix: _____ meaning: _____
   - suffix: _____ meaning: _____

Grammar, Usage, and Mechanics

A nonfiction reading & writing program • A nonfiction reading & writing program

First and Last (cont.)

8. **inattentiveness**: _____
   - stem: _____ meaning: _____
   - prefix: _____ meaning: _____
   - suffix: _____ meaning: _____

9. **deactivation**: _____
   - stem: _____ meaning: _____
   - prefix: _____ meaning: _____
   - suffix: _____ meaning: _____

10. **irrepressible**: _____
    - stem: _____ meaning: _____
    - prefix: _____ meaning: _____
    - suffix: _____ meaning: _____

Use the ten words from the list above and on the previous page to fill in the appropriate blanks.

1. Have you ever wondered how many millions of people have existed since time began? They are _____.

2. The corporate office has a _____ toward hiring first-year college graduates.

3. The secretary has a cold, _____ disposition that intimidates those she serves.

4. In India there are many factories where women and children are made to work long hours in _____ conditions with very low pay.

5. When I was questioned about my class behavior, my teacher was _____ toward my honest explanation.

6. The astronauts were on stand-by until something could be done to stop a steam leak in the rocket's main thruster. The scientists were beginning to fear another delay or the _____ of the rocket altogether.

7. The museum claimed to have an authentic Model T Ford, but when the public learned that the car was a reproduction, the museum acknowledged its _____ of the truth.

8. Restrained in hand and ankle cuffs, the criminal violently threw himself at anyone near him. He was _____, so the police finally had to administer a tranquilizer to calm him.

9. After working all day, she came home to unwind, only to realize she had forgotten to purchase tonight's dinner. What an _____! Now she had to go out again.

10. The boy was so proud of his efforts to create a Web site for his school. He wanted to post all of the school's events for everyone to see, but at the monthly awards ceremony, the principal didn't even mention his hard work. Discouraged, the boy felt unappreciated, and the principal's _____ really bothered him.

Grammar, Usage, and Mechanics

New Words

Add prefixes and/or suffixes to the following base words to write three new words for each.

1. kind _____
2. honest _____
3. fortune _____
4. conform _____
5. complete _____
6. inspect _____
7. appoint _____
8. trust _____
9. joy _____
10. charge _____

Write three words that begin with each prefix.

1. bi- _____
2. over- _____
3. pre- _____
4. mis- _____
5. dis- _____
6. re- _____
7. in- _____
8. ir- _____
9. tele- _____
10. sub- _____
11. per- _____
12. de- _____
13. il- _____
14. trans- _____
15. an- _____
16. non- _____

Grammar, Usage, and Mechanics

Number Usage

Use the following guidelines when you need to include numbers in your writing.

1. Spell out any numbers or amounts less than one hundred that can be expressed in less than three words.
   examples: seventy-four dollars, one-fourth, ten million voters

2. Spell out the number if it begins a sentence, unless it is a year; however, try not to start a sentence with a number at all.
   faulty example: 1989 was the year the Dodgers won the World Series.
   revised: The Dodgers won the World Series in 1989.

3. Use numerals for numbers such as dates, ages, symbols (5' 2"), road destinations (I–30), street numbers, mileage, monetary amounts, measured periods of time (9 months), decimals, percentages, measured weights (6-ounce package), page numbers, hours followed by A.M. or P.M., addresses, identification numbers (Elizabeth I, Channel 2, Apollo 14) and scores (7 to 3).

4. Use a numeral and a dash for a compound modifier.
   examples: 180-lb. man; 4-day old baby; 4,000 foot bridge; 9-volt battery

5. Use words to express how much of something is needed or referenced.
   example: thirty-nine 2-inch pipes

   Do not use words, however, when the quantity is over 100.
   example: 187 6-foot boards

6. Numbers that correlate should be written in the same style.
   example: Three stores, each with 1 manager, 4 clerks, and 5 stockers, share one basic complex.

Grammar, Usage, and Mechanics

1, 2, 3, Go!

In the following sentences, use a colored pen or pencil to make any necessary corrections in the use of numbers. Rewriting the entire sentence is not necessary.

1. 247 pigs died in the flood.
2. I live at seventeen Main Street.
3. There is a seventy-five percent off sale at Mervyns.
4. I sold five hundred forty one tickets on my first day working at the amusement park.
5. He is celebrating his 98th birthday.
6. It takes 4 years to complete high school.
7. Henry the Eighth was the father of Queen Elizabeth the First.
8. They measured it to the nearest sixty-seven hundredths of an inch.
9. He lived in the 15th century.
10. I have $17, and it's burning a hole in my pocket!

Answer the following questions in complete sentences. If you do not know the answer, make a guess. Just write the numbers correctly!

1. In what year was your oldest grandparent born?
   _____

2. At what time are you dismissed from school?
   _____

3. How much did you weigh when you were born, and how long were you?
   _____

4. On what channel is your favorite television show?
   _____

5. How old were you when you started walking?
   _____

6. How tall are you now, and how tall do you think you will be when you have finished growing?
   _____

7. How many square feet is your home?
   _____

Grammar, Usage, and Mechanics

About Paragraphs

A **paragraph** usually ranges from about 100 to 250 words and relates to one central theme. Paragraphs require unity, coherence, and adequate development. Unity means each sentence within the paragraph has a single, clear purpose; it contributes to one central thought found in the topic sentence. The **topic sentence**, usually found at the beginning of the paragraph, introduces this central thought.

Coherence requires that the body of the paragraph is constructed of sentences that are connected in an orderly, clear way so that each sentence flows smoothly. To do this, transitions are needed. A **transition** is a word or phrase used to link one sentence to another. Here is a list of many common transitions.

- to specify addition: *again, also, and, and then, in addition, equally important, besides, in the first place, in the second, next, finally, last, moreover, too, furthermore*

- to specify cause and effect: *hence, accordingly, therefore, consequently, then, as a result, in short, truly, thus, thereupon*

- to specify comparison: *similarly, likewise, in a like manner, in comparison*

- to specify contrast: *in opposition, but, yet, still, on the other hand, however, nonetheless, after all, although, true, at the same time, in contrast, on the contrary, notwithstanding, even so, otherwise*

- to specify concession: *naturally, of course, admittedly*

- to specify place: *here, there, beyond, nearly, opposite to, adjacent to*

- to specify time: *after a while, afterwards, as long as, as soon as, at length, at last, at that time, meanwhile, now, in the past, later, in the meantime, presently, shortly, temporarily, soon, lately, until, when, while, immediately, thereafter*

- to specify purpose: *for this purpose, to this end, because, since, with this in mind*

- to specify result: *therefore, hence, as a result, consequently, thereupon, accordingly*

- to specify a summary: *in brief, in short, in conclusion, to conclude, as has been noted, to sum up, to summarize, on the whole, in other words*

- to specify special features, ideas, or examples: *for example, incidentally, in fact, for instance, indeed, in other words, to illustrate, in particular, specifically*

Grammar, Usage, and Mechanics

About Paragraphs (cont.)

Lastly, adequate development is necessary so that there are enough details, facts, evidence, examples, and reasons to give meaning and understanding to the topic of your paragraph. Here are some suggestions to remember when writing paragraphs.

- Do not write short paragraphs that are inadequately developed. If you notice that several of your paragraphs deal with similar topics, combine them into one longer paragraph. If they deal with different topics, they need to be expanded so the main thought of each is adequately developed.

- Be careful when you are uniting your sentences within a paragraph to stick to the topic. Do not introduce new topics or points of view at the end. Instead, write a concluding sentence which summarizes the central idea of your paragraph.

- Equally important, be sure your paragraph takes the reader in order from sentence to sentence without adding confusion by jumping from thought to unrelated thought. Write events in sequence, arranging facts logically, and do not omit main argumentative points.

- Do not use confusing words or words that are hard to understand, nor should you repeat obvious conclusions.

- Furthermore, avoid using a tone that is sarcastic, phony, or excessively enthusiastic. Also, beware of talking down to your reader, as this is insulting.

Grammar, Usage, and Mechanics

A nonfiction reading & writing program • A nonfiction reading & writing program

Beware of the Body Snatchers!

Written below is the topic and concluding sentence for five different paragraphs. Fill in the body (the main supporting details) for each one. Be sure to edit each paragraph for punctuation and to provide coherence, transitions, and adequate development. You will need to complete this activity on additional sheets of paper.

1. Student tardiness causes real problems in the classroom.

   In short, the hassles caused by tardy students must be eradicated.

2. The city should allocate more money for skateboard parks.

   Consequently a portion of our city's collected taxes should be spent on our youth in the form of skateboard parks.

3. Due to the growing trend in health-conscious teens, all school cafeterias need to add a produce and salad bar to their menus.

   Since healthy eating is a concern for teens today, it only makes sense to add a vegetable and fruit bar in school cafeterias.

4. The problem with many parents of teenagers is that they impose too many rules.

   Most parents just need to relax and let us kids grow up without so many restrictions.

5. The accident on the soccer field was caused entirely by careless and negligent referees.

   Since the referees did not pay attention to the care of the players, a terrible accident occurred, and the referees are at fault.

   (Describe the "accident" as if you were a witness. Tell, in detail, what you saw, what you heard, what the conditions were, and how the referees might have been careless. Be creative in this exercise. Make up details and pay specific attention to smooth, flowing, orderly sentences. Focus on transitional words that indicate time and additions.)

Grammar, Usage, and Mechanics

Entirely Irrelevant and Out of Order

Each topic sentence is accompanied by a set of statements below it. Some of them are relevant to the topic and some are not. Eliminate the irrelevant ones, and organize and restructure the rest into an effective paragraph. You will need another sheet of paper to do so.

I. Given a choice, I would rather get a job than be a babysitter when I turn sixteen.

1. I am more interested in a good paying job when I turn sixteen than I am in babysitting.

2. I can earn more with a job than I can as a babysitter.

3. Some of the children that I have babysat in the past have been really hard to manage.

4. I have to consider the bad points of each type of job: kids can be brats and the public can be rude.

5. Opportunities for advancement are greater in the regular work force.

6. My cousin's first job as a waitress ensured a wallet full of cash from tips.

7. Babysitting only pays a couple of dollars an hour.

8. To me, it's all about money, and the work force pays better than babysitting does.

II. The school week should be reduced to four longer days per week.

1. School is boring: it's just the same old thing every day, and there's so much homework.

2. My teachers each think their class is the only one we students have; they give us more homework than we possibly can do.

3. Personally, five days is just too long for me. I get burned out, and I think my teachers do, too.

4. My dad has a four-day a week job, working ten hours per day.

5. We teens need more rest time since we're growing, and an extra day is all we ask.

6. Eight school hours for four days may be a bit too long, but we'll sacrifice for a longer weekend.

7. Teens are not adults yet, so we still need time to have fun and be with friends in a non-educational environment.

8. A four-day school week would really benefit us kids.

Grammar, Usage, and Mechanics

A nonfiction reading & writing program • A nonfiction reading & writing program

Summaries and Outlines

A **summary** is a brief retelling of a piece of writing. It includes only the highlights and important facts, written in the writer's own words. (It is also an excellent way to study.) A summary's purpose is to feature the author's central ideas. Written in simple sentences, a summary reduces the written piece until only the main ideas and most significant details remain.

An **outline** is a more organized and even less wordy type of summary. However, it can be used to construct a written piece as well to summarize it. Its pupose it to guide the writer in creating an organizational working plan, allowing for the logical and orderly development of the writer's subject.

To construct an outline, use Roman numerals to number the main ideas. Use capital letters to list brief facts or subtopics under each main idea. Numbers are used to list further information under the letters. Use a consistent method for numbering and indenting your headings and subheadings, as in this model:

  I.
     A.
        1.
        2.
     B.
  II.
(And so forth.)

Each Roman numeral designates a paragraph because each one has a different main idea. The capital letters and numbers list the information necessary to support the topic within each paragraph. Admittedly, there may be several numbers under each capital letter, indicating a need to break the written work into more paragraphs. Following is an example of a complete outline:

Title: Buying a Skateboard

  I. Sources that sell skateboards
     A. stores
     B. private ads
     C. garage sales
  II. Choosing the skateboard
     A. brand names
     B. unknown names
     C. criteria for choice
        1. condition of the board
        2. style of the board
        3. type of wheels
        4. price of the board
  III. Financing to buy the board
     A. doing chores
     B. garage sale
     C. trading something
     D. babysitting
     E. odd jobs

Grammar, Usage, and Mechanics

Outspoken Outlines

Construct a complete outline on another sheet of paper for one of the titles suggested below.

1. How to Build a Soapbox Racer
2. How to Bake a Cake
3. The Qualities of a Good Teacher
4. What My Parents Should Change and Why
5. Television Violence
6. The Qualities of a Great Youth Organization
7. Misleading Television Commercials
8. The Qualities of a True Friend
9. Things That Make Me Happy
10. My Life Ten Years From Now
11. How To Train a Dog
12. The Best Way To Learn Math
13. Planning a Great Vacation
14. Why the _____ Are the Best Team Ever
15. What Makes Me the Person I Am

Note: Keep in mind as you start your outline that good organization comes from keeping your purpose (title) clearly in mind and from arranging your ideas in an orderly way.

Grammar, Usage, and Mechanics

A nonfiction reading & writing program • A nonfiction reading & writing program

Compositions and Essays

Good writing requires thoughtful planning. A composition, or essay, is a paper written on a single subject that sometimes presents the author's views. It needs to be carefully prepared so that what is meant by the author is clear to the readers.

Follow the list of writing steps below as a guide to structured writing.

1. Select a subject and limit it so that you can handle the assignment in the time and space given. For example, the topic *Dishonesty* is too vague. Try instead, for example, *Dishonesty Between Friends*.

2. Decide on your purpose. Will your writing be expository (explaining to and informing your readers about the subject), persuasive (convincing your readers to believe and act as you do by appealing to their emotions and/or common sense), descriptive (sharing with your readers an impression that something has made on you), or narrative (telling your readers about an event)?

3. Create a thesis statement, the sentence that becomes the controlling idea and purpose of your paper. It is an introductory summary of your entire paper.

4. Make a rough list of ideas, details, evidence, and facts that support your thesis.

5. Construct these ideas into a well-ordered outline. Eliminate those ideas which do not belong.

6. Write a good opening statement to capture your reader's interest, including such information as interesting facts, unusual details, a firm statement of opinion, or a brief incident that leads directly into your main topic.

7. Begin your first draft, and don't lose momentum by letting problems with vocabulary frustrate you. Let your outline guide you. Add interesting facts and examples to make your subject come alive.

8. Revise your paper. Polish the sentences and paragraphs by considering the word selection, clarity, and unity. Be sure you end your paper with a brief summary that reminds your readers of the major points you have made regarding your thesis statement.

9. Take a break from your paper. Come back and edit it later with fresh eyes. If possible, have someone else edit it, too.

10. Revise your work as needed and write the final draft.

Challenge

Using your outline from the previous page, write a composition. Follow the preceding list of steps to do so.

Grammar, Usage, and Mechanics

Research Papers

A research paper differs from a composition in that it requires notetaking from several sources. It is not based on opinion, but solely on facts, which must be verifiable. You must carefully document how you obtain your results and evidence, and everything must be accurate and reliable.

Begin your research report by choosing a specific topic that is not too broad (requiring mountains of research and notetaking) and that can be found in several sources. Next, search for materials that are pertinent to your subject to prepare your preliminary bibliography: a list of articles, books, encyclopedias, newspaper reports, and the like. You can find these at the library.

After accumulating some books and articles, skim through them. Determine which aspects of the topic you wish to pursue. Limit areas of the topic that are too broad. Begin to write a rough outline, indicating which resource to use for each section and where you need to find more data.

Here is an example of a rough outline:

I. Worldwide Hunger—*Encyclopedia Britannica*
    A. War—*TIME* Magazine (give month and year)
    B. *Famine*—book by J. Smith
    C. Overpopulation—get more data
    D. Political takeovers—find a book

II. World Relief Funds—find list of these
    A. World Vision Program—find pamphlet at home
    B. Project Mercy—get info.

III. Future Relief—?

IV. Past Failures—?

These preliminary notes can help you organize your first draft and remember where you found the information. Being a rough outline, it will naturally be rewritten with new, more detailed information that will be found as you continue to research. The purpose, as with the writing of compositions and essays, is to guide and help you refine your thinking along the lines of the topic so that you create an organized final paper.

Your next trip to the library should be to look for books through the subject catalog (which is computerized in many libraries). Gather them and skim through one or two chapters. Do not waste time reading through books or articles which may turn out to be useless. (Note: Do make bibliography cards for each book or article so that they can be easily found on return trips to the library. Besides, they are a necessary component in the documentation of your evidence.) Once you have found all the books and articles for your research paper and have made a bibliography for each, you will need to take extensive notes. Be sure you know the source from which you took your notes. Unless you plan to quote your source (and if you do, put quotation marks around it) summarize what you read in your own words. Next, organize your notes as you have in your outline. Then write the paper using correct grammar, punctuation, sentence order, and effective transitions between sentences to unify key ideas.

Grammar, Usage, and Mechanics

A nonfiction reading & writing program • A nonfiction reading & writing program

Research Assignment

Choose one of the following topics on which to write a complete research outline, bibliography, and report.

1. Why was Joan of Arc burned at the stake?
2. What were the causes of the 1930's Dustbowl?
3. Who was Jesse James?
4. Tell the history of women's right to vote.
5. Tell the history of the settlers of Roanoke Island.
6. Who was Cleopatra?
7. Who actually discovered America before Columbus?
8. Tell the theories of dinosaur extinction.
9. Why did Adolph Hitler gain power in Germany?
10. Give the reasons and history for Operation Desert Storm.
11. Tell the events of the 1972 Munich Olympics.
12. Explain current special effect techniques in the movie industry.
13. How did man first come to land on the moon?
14. Explain how the first automobile came to be invented.
15. What is the purpose and history of the Nobel Peace Prize?
16. How did the western system of time and the calendar come to be invented?
17. Who is Rosa Parks and why is she important to American history?
18. Tell the events leading to and stemming from the bombing of Hiroshima, Japan.
19. Explain the system by which laws are passed in the United States federal government.
20. Tell the history of the construction of Paris' Notre Dame cathedral.

Grammar, Usage, and Mechanics

Answer Key

page 5

1. My Uncle James isn't a professional, but he can dance better than anyone I know.
   reason: The two clauses must be joined together with a comma and a conjunction.

2. Katie will attend swim lessons and bring her own swim accessories.
   OK. (No comma is needed since Katie is the subject for both verbs, "will attend" and "bring.")

3. Because their son was hospitalized, the parents also spent the night in the hospital.
   reason: The subordinate clause, " . . . son was hospitalized," cannot stand alone. It needs a comma to separate itself from the main clause.

4. I cannot believe my parents have imposed a telephone curfew on me; I can only talk for an hour a day.
   reason: The two complete sentences must be separated with punctuation.

5. He was late and that made me nervous.
   OK. (No comma is needed since the main clause comes first and the subordinate clause is added after the word *and*.)

6. The principal will be at the meeting tomorrow; however, the vice-principal will still be in the office.
   reason: The transitional word "however" must be set off by a semi-colon and a comma because it interrupts and separates both sentences.

7. The sixteen-year-old boy has had three accidents in four months; his insurance rates are high.
   reason: A semi-colon separates the two sentences, whereas a colon introduces a list or an important point.

8. The parade marchers were hot and sweaty; nonetheless, they were required to continue their one-mile course.
   reason: The transitional word "nonetheless" must be set off by a semi-colon and a comma because it interrupts and separates both sentences.

9. She couldn't decide which outfit to wear to the party; her clothes were strewn all over the floor.
   reason: The two complete sentences must be separated

10. After high school he has the option of going to college with a scholarship; on the other hand, he could play for a major league baseball team.
    reason: The transition "on the other hand" must be set off by a semi-colon and a comma because it interrupts and separates both sentences.

11. The toddlers played nicely until one took a toy belonging to the other.
    OK. (No comma is needed because the main clause comes first.)

12. The supermarket burnt down last night; the market across town is in business however.
    reason: The two complete sentences must be separated with punctuation.

13. If you train a horse well, it can do many tricks.
    reason: A comma is needed because the subordinate clause comes first and cannot stand by itself.

14. Some people believe that Humpty Dumpty fell off a wall; on the other hand, he may have been pushed.
    reason: The transition "on the other hand" must be set off by a semi-colon and a comma because it interrupts and separates both sentences.

15. The driving age for most states is sixteen years old; however, some states require kids to wait until they turn eighteen.
    reason: The transition "however" must be set off by a semi-colon and then a comma.

page 6

Sentences will vary. An example for each is provided.

1. Cranky and exhausted, we came home after a two-hour drive from the beach.

2. It was our ever-patient neighbor who brought home our dogs after they were found loose.

Grammar, Usage, and Mechanics

Answer Key (cont.)

page 6 (cont.)

3. His mouth full of nails and his hammer swinging like a piece of machinery, the carpenter put together the child's toy box with amazing precision.
4. Frugal, the mother was only able to afford second-hand clothing for her baby at the consignment store, yet obtained a beautiful, hardly worn, extensive wardrobe.
5. Where is the P.E. teacher? He has rushed onto the field to assist an injured player.
6. With an achy body and pounding head, he was aware that he was in the beginning stages of illness.
7. Like a wheat field on a dry, windy day, the singer swayed back and forth to the rhythm of the song.
8. Quick to offer assistance, the mainland states helped the island of Hawaii after a tsunami caused much devastation.
9. Where will they meet their friends, now that the beach is closed due to an oil spill?
10. Running to the man she thought was her father, the child gave the stranger a hug.

page 8

Sentences will vary. Here is an example for each.

1. The boy approached the horse warily, but it saw the bridle in his hand. Sensing this, the boy stood still and they eyed each other for a tense moment. Then the boy sprang into action and quickly tossed the reins in the direction of the horse's head, only to miss. All that was left of this one opportunity was a trail of dust as the horse galloped away.
2. A friend of mine, who knows a lot about cars, sold me a vehicle with engine problems. Now I'm worried because I'm not sure what is wrong, and I don't have the money to fix it.
3. Be careful, when you sneak a piece of chewing gum in class, to hide it from your teacher and to avoid popping a sticky bubble on your nose.
4. I woke up early enough this morning, but I dawdled in the shower and at breakfast, and I couldn't make up my mind which outfit to wear; when the bus came, I was still in my underwear.

5. The space trip was a success, but the astronauts were kept in seclusion for weeks afterward for observation because of what the mad scientist, Dr. Stinkinbinder, tried to do. Why, he attempted to sabotage the whole space program by infecting the astronauts with highly infectious germs that he shot into outer space!

page 10

A. Sentences will vary. Here is an example for each.

1. Hilariously endowed with thinned hair, a freckled face, and stooped posture, the comedian imitated a beauty pageant queen.
2. The Jerry Lewis telethon has finally paid off! A local chemist has surprising and shocking news—he has found a cure for M.D.! The results will be simply mind-boggling.
3. Ridiculously dressed as an octopus and a giant clam, the students performed hilariously in the school talent show.
4. The canyon walls are reverberating with the thundering and clashing of the tremendous storm overhead.
5. The vicious, ferocious monster smashed cars and buildings as it chased after me in a blood-curdling nightmare.
6. Uncle Jethro's inheritance of six hound dogs, his brand-new furniture, and a million dollars all goes to me!

B. Sentences will vary. Here is an example for each.

1. Parents enrolling kindergarten students need shot records and complete school paperwork
2. My teacher not only works full-time, but she does her own housework, involves herself in the P.T.A., and goes to graduate school.
3. Our school committee voted to replace our portables with ones that have more room and air-conditioning.
4. To be a good policeman, one must uphold the law, be level headed amidst unpredicle circumstances, like to help others, and keep in good physical shape.

Grammar, Usage, and Mechanics

Answer Key (cont.)

page 10 (cont.)

5. Our Boy Scout leader is effective because he's honest, funny, and speaks better than anyone I know.

page 12

Revised sentences will vary. An example is provided for each.

1. FP: The magician's first trick was one with a length of rope.
2. F: I think we should either ignore the gang or leave quickly.
3. FPR: Jake's bunny, with ear mites, is always scratching itself.
4. MC: Every effort the foreigner made to be understood got him more confused.
5. F: The dentist finally called me into his office for a conference about my dental health.
6. FP: Another kind of crime is one in which a person is dishonest before the judge and jury. This is called perjury.
7. MC: Having spent large sums on campaign endorsements, the government has fewer resources to help the sick and elderly.
8. R: When Lewis and Clark first gazed upon the canyon, their mouths dropped in awe.
9. FPR: The brightly colored rainbows shined over the rich field of flowers.
10. FP: As the center for most T.V. studios, Hollywood is the city where most actors, actresses, and models yearn to go.

page 15

1. After leaving Newport Beach, we sailed west toward Catalina Island for our summer vacation with my cousins and Uncle John.
2. Dr. Martin Luther King, Jr., first gained public awareness as a leader in the Civil Rights sit-ins in the South.
3. The U.S. Congress is made of the House of Representatives and the Senate, which is elected every two years, to pass national laws.
4. I took a chemistry course in my freshman year in high school in Nebraska, and I was a college graduate student five years later.
5. Last summer we attended Vacation Bible School at Grant Park, Northwest of Grant Elementary School.
6. Though I've never seen *Phantom of the Opera*, my grandmother told me that the African American man who plays the Phantom is incredibly talented.
7. We went to hear the choir at the community college last Saturday. Some of the songs they sang were traditional, some were from popular movies, and a few were patriotic. They sang a wonderful rendition of "The Battle Hymn of the Republic."
8. I'll never forget last Labor Day when my sister was actually in labor giving birth to her first-born son at San Antonio Hospital.
9. I'm driving the new Ford to Ralph's Market to purchase Coca-Cola, toilet paper, soda crackers, Oreo Cookies, and Fruit Loops.
10. My father is the president of Toys R' Us. He can get great deals on things like Pokemon videos, Game Boy cartridges, skate boards, bikes and Mattel products.

page 20

There is some room for variation in the punctuation. Here are examples of correctly punctuated sentences.

1. Many young boys hope to become professional sportsmen; however, few realize the amount of work necessary—not to mention the luck involved in becoming a success.
2. Some people feel that American public schools should only be taught in English, not Spanish; nevertheless, some schools do still have waivers for bilingual education—not just English.
3. When the test was placed in front of him, he realized—dreading his upcoming report card—how much more he should have studied.
4. The vice president of the company boasts that he is self-made and self-educated, but his boasting, which occurs every time he opens his mouth, shows his self-centeredness.
5. There are three types of government: the federal, state, and local.
6. I have to be at the Chess Club meeting after

©Teacher Created Materials, Inc.

Grammar, Usage, and Mechanics

Answer Key (cont.)

page 20 *(cont.)*

school; we're taking pictures for our class bulletin board, the Tyler School yearbook, and *The Evening Press Newspaper*.

7. Delighted to hold his one-day-old son, the new father burst into tears of joy—amazed beyond words at the priceless miracle he'd received.

8. After selling off all his old things at the garage sale, he sat and thought about what he had gotten rid of: the books his grandmother had bought him, his race car sets, the train set his dad and he had bought together, and model cars—everything sentimental; was it really worth the small amount of money he had made, he wondered.

9. It's easy to borrow money; it's much more difficult to pay it back.

10. Some say that America is taking over the world—not necessarily with world power and force, but with the use of media through television, film, radio, and the press.

page 21

A. "Where today are the Pequot? Where are the Narragansett . . . and many other once powerful tribes of our people? They have vanished before the avarice and the oppression of the White Man, as snow before a summer sun.

Will we let ourselves be destroyed in our turn without a struggle, give up our homes, our country bequeathed to us by the Great Spirit, the graves of our own dead . . . ? I know you will cry with me,

'Never! Never!'"

B. James W. Marshall was the first man to find gold in California in 1848 at Sutter's Mill. Word of the find eventually spread like wildfire. "Gold! Gold! There's gold in them, there hills!" prospectors shouted. San Francisco virtually became a ghost town overnight. Miners could earn as much as seventy-five dollars a day, as opposed to the six dollars a month they had been earning on average before the strike. Entrepreneurs asked themselves if selling supplies might be more profitable than mining for gold. These entrepreneurs got rich overnight by selling flour, sugar, coffee, shovels, picks, pans, and more to the miners at incredibly high prices. In addition, gold fever swept the nation with epidemic speed, and California's population rose drastically because of it. Was this one of America's most noted periods in history? Some historians believe so.

page 22

1. I've seen Broadway's *Cats* twice, and I still find its musical choreography exciting, well done, and original.

reasons: The apostrophe in *I've* shows the contraction *I have*. The name of a play should be capitalized and have no apostrophe because it does not show possession. A comma should be placed after *twice* to indicate a natural pause and break between the two complete sentences. *I* should be capitalized. Remove the apostrophe from *its* because it is not a contraction. There should also be a comma after *done* because it separates words in a series. Finally, there should be a period at the end of a declarative sentence.

2. People of all races must learn to live and work together without prejudice; otherwise, this country will fail.

This sentence is correct as it is.

reasons: The semi-colon is placed correctly in front of the transitional word, the transitional word is followed by a comma, and the period is placed correctly at the end of this declarative sentence.

3. I wondered why I received an unexpected letter from the director of the Internal Revenue Service. Could I have done something wrong, I pondered. It turned out simply to be a reminder to sign the form I had sent.

reasons: *Unexpected* should not be hyphenated. *Director* is a common noun and no capitalization is necessary. *Internal Revenue Service* is a proper noun and should be capitalized. "Service" ends a declarative sentence and should be followed by a period. A period should be placed at the end of a declarative sentence, and *I pondered* makes the sentence declarative, not interrogative. (It is an indirect question.)

Grammar, Usage, and Mechanics

Answer Key (cont.)

page 22 *(cont.)*

4. Does anyone know who said, "I've never met a man I didn't like"? I think it was Will Rogers, a friend to all men.

reasons: A comma is used to separate a quotation tag from a quotation. Quotation marks are used at the beginning and end of a direct quote. *I've* should be capitalized, and the apostrophe shows the contraction for *I have*. *Didn't* requires an apostrophe between *n* and *t* for the contraction *did not*. The question mark is placed outside the quotes because the quoted material is not an interrogative sentence. The comma after Will Rogers sets off the appositive.

5. Our family enjoys trips to Laughlin, Nevada, for several reasons: the boating and skiing on the river, the gambling, and the dining at the buffets. My father likes gambling in all the casinos: Harrahs, the Flamingo, the Hilton—you know the rest. He often wins the jackpots. I call him "The Jackpot King" when he plays the slot machines at all those different casinos. The biggest amount he ever won was $8,000, and he didn't even share a penny of it with me!

reasons: *Trips* needs no apostrophe since it is not possessive. There should be a comma between a city and state as well as after the state if the sentence continues. A colon is used to introduce a list. Commas are used to separate items in a list. A period is placed at the end of a declarative sentence. A dash is placed at the end of a sentence to add an extra thought. Quotation marks are used around a special title, and the title is capitalized. A dollar sign and comma are inserted to indicate money and the thousands place. Also, add a comma after $8,000 to separate the two clauses. An exclamation point is placed at the end of an exclamatory sentence.

page 25

Proper	Common/Concrete	Abstract	Collective
Harry Potter	principal	capacity	committee
Albert Einstein	senator	bureaucracy	society
Yukatan	galaxy	burden	convoy
Koran	comedian	occurrence	clique
Aborigine	critic	obsession	multitude
	correspondence	heritage	impression

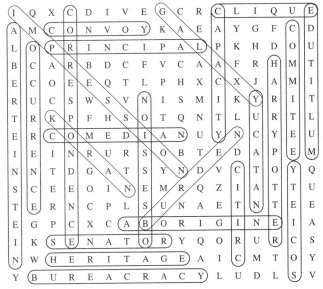

page 27

A. Answers will vary.
B. Some answers will vary.

1. The child replied, "I can do it all by myself."
2. Sherry got the phone numbers of two boys at school. She wanted to go out with one of them Saturday night, but she wasn't sure which one to ask. So, she asked a neighbor to help. "Whom should I ask to go out with me this Saturday?" she asked her neighbor.
3. Mr. Jones stepped on the scale at the doctor's office. It read 225 pounds. Mr. Jones could not believe his eyes. "I guess I've gained a few too many. This body of mine isn't growing any taller any more, is it? It's just a lot wider. It's my wife's rich cooking. What can I do?"

The doctor replied, "You are going to have to lose this weight by dieting and exercising. No one can do it for you. You'll have to do it yourself.

Grammar, Usage, and Mechanics

Answer Key (cont.)

page 27 (cont.)

4. It was late at night. My family stayed up to watch a movie. Suddenly there was a knock at the door. Dad called out, "Who is it?" No one answered; there wasn't a single sound. We didn't think much of it until the same thing happened again a few minutes later. Who could it be bothering us this late at night, we wondered. Someone was really scaring us now. After the third knock, in about twenty minutes, my dad yelled out, "I have just called the police! They are on the way, right now!" Whoever it was must have left right then because he or she never bothered us again.

page 30
1. Their family has lived there longer than ours.
2. It was she who was elected prom queen.
3. When we heard the tap on the window, we knew it was he.
4. We found John and her at the park.
5. Whom do you wish to replace, him or me?
6. Our rude neighbors reported him as well as me to the police for something that wasn't even done by us.
7. Yours is the car whose front end is parked on our property.
8. You and they were in the play we saw last night.
9. Janie was the girl for whom all the seventh and eighth grade boys voted.
10. In the distance the man resembled my grandfather. Shocked, I just stared, almost thinking it was he.

page 32
The listed words are verbs.
1. yearn, turn, spurn, earn, learn, burn, adjourn, churn
2. daze, amaze, faze, graze, gaze, laze, raise, stays
3. gasp, clasp, grasp, rasp
4. sever
5. leave, cleave, believe, grieve, heave, receive, retrieve, weave, achieve
6. devour, cower, dower, sour
7. stare, bare, care, dare, declare, glare, fare, tear, wear, spare, ensnare, flare, bear

page 33
The verb in each sentence is listed. Alternative verbs will vary.
1. compiled
2. has deteriorated
3. indulged
4. scampered
5. has been inspired
6. saturated
7. prohibit
8. lauded
9. subverted
10. defeated

page 36
Sentences will vary.

page 37
purple (proper) = Russian, Renaissance, Victorian, Panamanian, Mongolian, Communist

yellow (indefinite) = inferior, several, various, major, less, more, additional, further

red (possessive) = theirs, his, ours, hers, my, yours, their, its

green (demonstrative) = that, those, this, these

blue (common) = colossal, elegant, immobile, vigorous, moody, interfering, cynical, commendable, ludicrous, concealed, shady

orange (adverbs) = approximately, eventually, totally, gradually, always, well, very, too

uncolored (neither adjective nor adverb) = discord, aperture, ambush, acne, aviation, discourage, populace, quarrel, establish, mobility, bicycle

page 38
1. Adam is the taller of the two boys.
2. The Rose Parade floats rolled majestically down the street.
3. He is the laziest boy I've ever met.

Grammar, Usage, and Mechanics

Answer Key (cont.)

page 38 (cont.)

4. American cars always break down.
5. The play is tragic.
6. The counselor gave the arguing couple a disapproving look.
7. The wild roller coaster dips and turns in a thrilling ride.
8. The wreck wasn't nearly as bad as it could have been if the driver had not been driving so responsibly.
9. He looked suspiciously at me!
10. A teacher works considerably harder than many other professions for less pay.
11. She worked hastily on her chores so she could finish and visit a sickly (or *sick*) friend.
12. The outdated school campus severely irritated the students. *or* The outdated school campus greatly irritated the students.
13. I came upon quite a noisy scene as I walked down the street: two dogs barking loudly at a scared cat up a tree.
14. The construction worker exhausted himself too much in the hot sun and passed out from the extreme heat.
15. "Either clean this room, young man, or spend the next week without any television!" his mother yelled irately.

page 40

Sentences will vary.

page 41

verbs = impoverish, revere, intimidate, parry

nouns = tessellation, integrity, dross, panacea

adjectives = innocent, Cubans, reverent, insubordinate, innocuous

adverbs = tonight, credibly, selfishly, nevermore

conjunctions = and, nor, but, or, yet, so, because

interjections = oops, yuck, wow

pronouns = myself, you, herself, it, mine, I

prepositions = beside, during, for, in, through, from

page 43

1. arrangement; Rule # 3
2. pleasure; Rule # 2
3. conveyance; Rule # 9
4. untying; Rule # 7
5. replacement; Rule # 3
6. preserving; Rule # 2
7. crankiness; Rule # 8
8. persuing; Rule # 2
9. statement; Rule # 5
10. generalized; Rule # 2
11. renouncing; Rule # 4
12. duly; Rule # 6
13. association; Rule # 2
14. business; Rule # 8
15. changeable; Rule # 3
16. changing; Rule # 4
17. conceivable; Rule # 2
18. eightieth; Rule # 8
19. courageous; Rule # 3
20. correct: variety, anxiety, deceit, fiend, impatient, skein, receipt, perceive, priest, besiege, neighbor, foreign, financier, seizure

page 46

1. I believe it's admirable to be peaceful during times of unnecessary ungovernable agitation.
2. The management has busied itself in persuading the corporation to raise the salaries of the secretaries.
3. I am dissatisfied with the outcome of my recent surgeries; the scars are really noticeable. I feel the doctors deceived me by assuring me there would be no disfigurement.
4. She admitted that she truly benefited from the judgement that accidentally freed her from all liabilities in the civil case.
5. The ambitious young executive is also an aspiring politician.
6. The little actress has become quite ostentatious, and it's all because her unscrupulous mother sees to it that her daughter gets whatever roles she finds desirable at any cost.

Grammar, Usage, and Mechanics

Answer Key (cont.)

page 46 *(cont.)*

7. The location of the churches the missionaries are visiting is confusing. The dirt roads are not serviceable, being holey and unstable. The surrounding area is steep and mountainous, seemingly unsuitable for any buildings besides huts. Perplexed, the emissaries are seeking the assistance of the local inhabitants to find the correct way to the establishments.

8. The preschoolers in our school were acting very cranky one day. I was assisting in their room, and they were about to drive me crazy. I mean it! At lunchtime, one little tot complained hysterically that he wanted a carrot stick, not a carrot. What's the difference? Then when we were singing, another youngster was so unruly; he kept pulling people's hair, moving all over when he should have been in one place, and screeching rather than singing. I was despairing of ever getting through that class. When it was finally over the teacher approached me and commended me for my patience. I guess I managed a lot better than I had previously thought.

page 49

1. OK
2. #3; There are a few bouncing balls and jump ropes left in the ball room.
3. #1; The first ten customers were to receive a gift certificate.
4. #7; The majority is angry about the mayor's decision.
5. OK
6. #8; The point of the conversation is differences between girls and boys and how to get along with one another.
7. #5; In the garage there are my dad's hot rods.
8. #4; Neither the children nor the babysitter was to eat the popsicles in the freezer.
9. #6; The chewy candies in my candy bag are the only ones left that get stuck in my teeth.
10. #2; Every policeman and fireman came to make his appearance at the community cook-off.

page 50

1. When the bus overturned in the ditch, it was later learned that the occupants had <u>broken</u> many bones.
2. Upon interviewing a witness of the accident, the public ascertained that there <u>was</u> no one else at the scene to help at the time.
3. The witness <u>did</u> what he could to help, but it <u>wasn't</u> enough. There <u>were</u> too many injured people and it would have <u>taken</u> him all day to free everyone from the wreckage and rubble.
4. Finally someone <u>saw</u> the wreck and <u>came</u> to help. The work would have been exhausting for the two "good Samaritans" if a trucker hadn't also <u>seen</u> the crash and <u>gone</u> for help.
5. The emergency response team arrived soon after and <u>went</u> to work freeing the rest of the crash victims.

page 53

 The alumni of O'Grady High School—they call themselves the O'Grady's Graduates—went on several wildlife seeing fieldtrips this past summer. Many people participated. Three members of the Humphries' family also attended. (Mr. Humphries is our school's principal, by the way.) During their many rendezvous, they enjoyed seeing salmon runs, a fish hatchery, and mixed varieties of fish, wild moose, deer, and geese.

 On one such trip, a few of the women and their children wandered off in search of an outhouse. They witnessed a strange phenomenon. Some mice were seen baring their teeth at one another. The women talked amongst themselves about the oddity of such behavior and made an analysis: the creatures must have simply been afraid of the passers-by and were, in all probability, reacting to them.

Grammar, Usage, and Mechanics

Answer Key (cont.)

page 54
1. babies'
2. boss's
3. empresses
4. roping
5. preferred, glasses
6. happiest, burying
7. Mosses, owner's
8. admitted, forgetting, preference
9. baby's, blanket's, spots, spots, it's
10. Cooks, radios, echoes, neighbor's

pages 57 and 58
Definitions may vary somewhat.
1. disinclination: unwillingness
   - stem: incline   meaning: to influence
   - prefix: dis-   meaning: not, away
   - suffix: -tion   meaning: state or condition
2. innumerable: too many to be counted
   - stem: numerate   meaning: number
   - prefix: in-   meaning: into/not
   - suffix: -able   meaning: capable of being
3. unsympathetic: not caring
   - stem: sympathy   meaning: mutual understanding between people
   - prefix: un-   meaning: not
   - suffix: -ic   meaning: pertaining to, like
4. substandardized: less than adequate
   - stem: standard   meaning: measure of value, criteria
   - prefix: sub-   meaning: under
   - suffix: -ized   meaning: made
5. impersonal: not personal; emotionless
   - stem: person   meaning: human being
   - prefix: im-   meaning: not
   - suffix: -al   meaning: relating to
6. misrepresentation: incorrect, dishonest depiction
   - stem: represent   meaning: to stand for, portray
   - prefix: mis-   meaning: wrong
   - suffix: -ation   meaning: state or condition
7. inconvenience: causing trouble, a bother
   - stem: convenient   meaning: suited to one's needs
   - prefix: in-   meaning: not
   - suffix: -ce   meaning: state of
8. inattentiveness: negligent, heedless
   - stem: attentive   meaning: heedful, observant, courteous
   - prefix: in-   meaning: not
   - suffix: ness-   meaning: state of being
9. deactivation: to render inactive
   - stem: activate   meaning: set in motion, organize
   - prefix: de-   meaning: from, down
   - suffix: -tion   meaning: state or condition
10. irrepressible: not able to be controlled
    - stem: repress   meaning: hold back, restrain
    - prefix: ir-   meaning: not
    - suffix: -ible (same as -able)   meaning: capable of being

1. innumerable
2. disinclination
3. impersonal
4. substandardized
5. unsympathetic
6. deactivation
7. misrepresentation
8. irrepressible
9. inconvenience
10. inattentiveness

page 59
Words will vary.

Grammar, Usage, and Mechanics

Answer Key (cont.)

page 61
1. Two hundred forty seven pigs died in the flood.
2. I live at 17 Main Street.
3. There is a 75% off sale at Mervyns.
4. I sold 541 tickets on my first day working at the amusement park.
5. He is celebrating his ninety-eighth birthday.
6. It takes four years to complete high school.
7. Henry VIII was the father of Queen Elizabeth I.
8. They measured it to the nearest .67 of an inch.
9. He lived in the fifteenth century.
10. I have seventeen dollars, and it's burning a hole in my pocket!

The rest of the sentences will vary.

page 65

I. Eliminate sentences 3 and 4. Sentence 6 can be eliminated or incorporated.

Here is one possible paragraph:

    Given my choice I would rather get a job than be a babysitter when I turn sixteen. Basically, I am more interested in a good paying job than I am with babysitting, which pays quite a few less dollars per hour than minimum wage does. In addition, opportunities for advancement are greater in the work force. Therefore, in a couple of years, if I stick with the same job, I can earn a raise and a chance for a promotion. That is something that would never happen if I chose to babysit. In short, it's all about money to me, and since the work force pays better and has better opportunities than babysitting does, that's what I want to do.

II. Omit sentences 1 and 2. Sentence 4 can be eliminated or incorporated.

Here is one possible paragraph:

    The school week should be reduced to four longer days per week. I know what I'm talking about, because my dad once had a job with a four-day work week, working ten hours per day. Our family really liked it because of the extra time we spent together as a family on his three-day weekend, and my dad liked it because he didn't get burned out. Now we kids could benefit in the same way. We could spend more time with our friends in a non-educational setting and have fun together, just like my family did, and we wouldn't get burned out quite so easily. Speaking of burn out, don't teachers need the same option? You get burned-out just as easily as we kids do. I believe we would gladly sacrifice and go to school eight full hours a day for four days in order to have a longer weekend. After all, we teens need more rest-time, since we're still growing, and an extra day is all we're asking. This is not at the expense of our education, because we will still put in the same amount of hours as in a five-day school week. Please consider that a four-day school week would really benefit us kids as well as you teachers.